Breaking Through Special Needs:

The Ultimate Guide to Navigating Life as a Special Needs Parent

© 2020 Christine Astarita

All Rights Reserved.
No part of this publication may be reproduced, distributed, or transmitted in any form or by any means, including photocopying, recording, or other electronic or mechanical methods, without the prior written permission of the publisher, except in the case of brief quotations embodied in critical reviews and certain other noncommercial uses permitted by copyright law.

Publisher: Christine Astarita
1747-21 Veterans Memorial Highway, Islandia, NY 11749

Breaking Through Special Needs

We met Christine 3 years ago when she first opened her therapy practice. We were so excited that there was intensive physical therapy available for our son Howie. Before starting at Breakthrough Howie's physical progress was stagnant. Since he started with Christine Howie has begun to gain strength and his school therapist reported that she sees a big difference in strength and progress during therapy. Howie loves going to Breakthrough Intensive Physical Therapy. Christine is not just Howie's therapist she is like family to us now. She goes above and beyond therapy and helps all of the families in every way she can. Her support is valuable to us. We are so grateful that we found Christine and Breakthrough

Cynthia and Joe R

Christine has not only helped my daughter in gaining strength and balance via her PT sessions but she has also helped our family as a whole. With my son via Sibshops, and my husband and I by lending a sympathetic ear or helpful advice. Her dedication to the Special Needs Community goes far beyond Intensive Physical therapy and has touched us all as a family.

Kathy D.

My daughter Emerson met Christine in July 2014 and has been an integral part of her physical therapy journey. She is stronger, has better balance and enjoys working hard because Christine's approach to motivation is fun but firm. She takes into consideration the needs of our entire family by providing sibling support, parent support and informational events. We are extremely grateful to Christine and Breakthrough for the continued devotion to our family and community.

Patti W.

We met Christine in 2018 when Savvy was 3 years old and she was not happy to take part in physical therapy. If it wasn't for Christine's knowledge and encouragement we would have not return. She was able to show Savvy how it felt to sit up, crawl and walk! Savvy is now 6 and loves every minute at Breakthrough!

Cristina T.

I've heard my whole life that certain people will make an impact on you; leave an imprint in your heart and mind. There's been a few, but none the way Christine has for me. She's a special person. She truly believes in what she does and she does it with all of her heart and soul. I've become a better me by knowing her and watching her. She makes both

Breaking Through Special Needs

myself and my husband want to strive to be better parents, friends, and humans. I am grateful for crossing paths with Christine Astarita and for being on this journey with her.

Liz M.

Christine has had a tremendous impact on our daughter Maddie's life for the past 2 years. Her physical gains have been incredible. But more importantly, she has given my husband and I the most priceless gift that nobody could ever give us, and that's the hope that Maddie can one day be as independent as possible.

Liz C.

All my life I've been in many different forms of Physical Therapy, but Breakthrough, Christine and the staff there have been the best I've ever worked with. I am working on things physically that I never thought I'd be doing or working on, pushing myself to limits I never have before and having fun while doing it.

Henry L.

Breaking Through Special Needs

Breaking Through Special Needs

To all families with a special needs child, may you continue to treasure the small moments and little miracles in life that give you joy. You are the jack of all trades. I hope this book helps to guide you on your journey and gives you hope. You are not alone.

Breaking Through Special Needs

Contents

Introduction _____ 1

Being an Advocate _____ 8

Isolation Is Real _____ 22

Siblings Need Support Too _____ 33

Maintaining a Healthy Lifestyle _____ 58

Incorporating Home Exercises: For PT and General Fitness ___ 70

Lifting and Transfers _____ 76

Alternative Therapies _____ 96

The Legalities… From Someone Who Isn't A Lawyer _____ 102

Clinical FAQ's… _____ 106

Feel Good Stories _____ 116

Final Thoughts _____ 156

Breaking Through Special Needs

Introduction

I want to let you in on secret… I do not have a special needs child. So, you might be wondering why a therapist is writing a book for parents when I'm not directly in your shoes. But, I'll let you in on another secret… that has never stopped me from following my passion in life. My life's mission is to create a world in which special needs families' lives are positively impacted by the support I can give. It's not just about the children – though of course that's ultimately why I'm writing this and why you're diligently following along – it's also about you, the parents. Your journey is one of great patience, empathy, and love, and it really cannot be understated. I wrote this book to give you a shoulder to lean on and to provide support in times of need. I wrote this for your child's brothers and sisters – to give them some space to be understood and heard. This book is for the future of your entire family. I hope to draw from my experiences, the questions my clients have asked me, and the journey I've taken in my own life and career in order to help you access the best life for your special needs child, your other kids, the rest of your family… and of course, *you too.*

***

Let's start at the beginning. I never thought I would be a pediatric therapist. I thought it would be way too hard emotionally; I'd have to witness situations where children and young adults were dealt seemingly unfair cards in life and I didn't know if I could do that. In fact, I always told myself I'd like to be a therapist for the *New York Giants* – not kids – and that I wanted to be heavily involved in the sports physical therapy realm, perhaps owning my very own business and treating world class professional athletes. That used to be my dream, and looking back I cannot imagine why I ever wanted that – my life is so full and fulfilling now. That's not to say I may not have been happy helping athletes, of course, it's just that now each of my days is filled with a unique type of satisfaction. Dreams don't just change, mind you, and it took a 12 week clinical rotation with pediatrics in a special needs school district in New Jersey to blindside me and totally *change my life.*

Breaking Through Special Needs

As with all things, change happens in the most unexpected ways. I distinctly remember a young, 20 year old man on that special rotation. At that time, he would have been graduating from high school soon. He had Spastic Quadriplegic Cerebral Palsy and drove himself around in a power wheelchair. Although he had difficulty getting himself around, he was able to verbally communicate some of the time. I had the welcome opportunity to work with him twice a week during my time there. Sadly, the young man came from a tough background and was currently living in a foster home. Prior to one particular session, the young man started to verbalize and repeat the words "Stop! Stop! Stop!", but we hadn't started the session yet. In fact, I was busy communicating the plan for the day with my Clinical Instructor. I immediately turned my attention to him and asked him what was wrong, if he was hurt, and what I could do to help him. To my astonishment, my Clinical Instructor stopped me. I was incredibly confused and just wanted to help the young man feel better. My CI explained that we needed to wait for him to stop yelling. So, despite my hesitation, I waited. I think my CI could feel my anguish, and so in her understanding way, she gave me some context. The young man had a troubled history, and prior to moving in with his foster family, he had been sexually abused by a family member. The yelling and upset he was going through was his way of working through the PTSD he carried with him. My heart broke.

It took everything in me not to cry at that very moment. And yet, I'm crying as I write this; it still hurts my heart just as much. I can never say for sure that a single moment changed the direction of my life forever, but if there was ever a moment that came close, it would be this one; what I experienced witnessing that young man working through his trauma changed me inexplicably. He had a significant impact on my life, though will never know it. During the course of his treatment, there were a few other moments that triggered events just like the one I described above, but the remainder of the times I worked with him, he was innocently and purely himself. He had a smile so incredibly wide, and he had an infectious laugh that could light up your heart. What struck me most was that he had an innocence about him that made me want to sit and talk with him for hours. He even laughed at my corny jokes and silly faces or voices. He allowed me to be one hundred percent of myself without judgement, and he created joy within whomever was with him. Who wouldn't be moved by this?

Breaking Through Special Needs

Let me tell you about one more experience that has had a significant impact on my life. Though the first pivoted my career path, the second cemented the choice. I was working at my second special needs job out of PT school, and had an evaluation on my schedule for a little two-and-a-half year old girl. Her medical history was complex, as she had suffered a hemorrhage in her brain, thereby causing her to have Hemiplegic (one sided) Cerebral Palsy. She was a beautiful little girl, and despite the fact that she didn't want to use the left side of her body for anything, she was incredibly cute. It was clear, however, that this little girl and her family needed help: as I took her through her evaluation, she CRIED. And when I say that she cried, please don't misunderstand me. I don't mean that she was just complaining and whining as a typical toddler may do. No, this was full-blown hysteria. I'm talking boogers, tears, pouting... the whole shebang. You get the picture, right? When I asked her mom if she was in pain, or if something had scared her... she replied with tears in her eyes. "No," she said, "it's just really hard for her to do this." I immediately understood both mom and baby were suffering, and in that moment another shift in my life occurred.

I started to take her through the developmental sequence, trying to see if she would activate her left side to help her hold positions or even get into positions herself. Yet, just holding hands and knees was so incredibly hard for her. My heart physically ached for this mother and her child. Her mother was desperate to help her daughter be the best version of herself, and this little girl was faced with challenges nobody should ever have to endure: both were living on pure hope and faith. I continued to work with this little girl in treatment sessions, and during each and every session there were tears. On several occasions, her mom even had to leave the room because it was too hard to see her little girl struggling the way she was. I empathized with both.

And yet – things improved! Soon she started to crawl! Then she started to stand! And then she started taking steps with a walker! She always worked for a purple lollipop at the end, and in so doing put a smile on everyone's faces. I'll never forget the day they came into the office and told me that they'd been practicing steps at home and she started taking a few of her own. I was now the one who wanted to burst into tears. We then set her up – I was behind her and her mom was in front for her – and I brought out the musical drum she loved. She held two drum sticks

Breaking Through Special Needs

in her hands for security, and she took fourteen steps to the drum on her own that day. I knew that neither of us would ever look back.

Fourteen steps.

Those fourteen steps turned into infinite steps. A few months later, she gained the ability to get up from the floor by herself. Over time, those steps turned into dancing around to Descendants music, performing karate, and getting to run into mom and dad's arms. It turned into her being more independent than every doctor told her she would be. It turned into her living a better quality of life and getting to experience life in an entirely different way. Each and every moment was a celebration. All of that crying and struggle was part of the journey. How lucky am I that I got to be part of that? I remind myself of this fact on a daily basis.

This family has become an important part of mine, and holds an extremely special place in my heart. It was one of the first times I had to experience many low moments with a family – we built our way up to the highs and achievements. Watching this little girl work through so much helped me gain an entirely new perspective on the little things. What do I mean by that? Well, the little things that we take for granted about our abilities every single day. She taught me to ask myself what is *my* purple lollipop? She taught me that I need to keep working towards my goals, even if it gets hard, so that I can achieve the life I dream of.

I am still lucky to be part of this family's journey as we continue to work together to help this beautiful girl be her best self. She is well on the road to being as independent as possible. I've had the ability to watch this little girl grow and become more independent; we've worked through the hard moments and shared in the achievements no matter how big or small they have been. And do you want to know the best part? They aren't the only family that I've gotten to do this with! And though this little girl will always hold a special place in my heart, as she – in many ways – shaped me into the therapist and business owner I am today, I can honestly say I am blessed to help families on a daily basis now. Ever since my clinical rotation with individuals like the young man and little girl, I've known that my mission and passion is to support kids like them, parents like hers, and to be a resource for the special needs community to draw upon.

Breaking Through Special Needs

As I continued to work within the community, I began noticing that every child I got the opportunity to be around was just the same: innocent, pure, and happy. Even when they weren't able to communicate with their voices, they were aware of everything going on around them; whether they "fake slept" to get out of doing work, or showed excitement when they did something for the first time. My experiences during my clinical rotation, and my interaction with all of the families I have had the opportunity to work with since, has created a sense of fulfillment that is unmatched. Why? Well, what is better than filling your heart with love while making a meaningful difference in the lives of those you treat? And what's better than being taught more than you could ever imagine from the people you help? I am being taught knowledge that goes way beyond physical therapy… I am being taught about life.

There is nothing better. Nothing.

If I'm honest, I could write forever about all of the specific instances that have changed my life in such a way that I followed this career path and pursued my passion. Being a pediatric PT, you don't go home at the end of the day and forget about work. You think about the child that took their first steps and how grateful you feel to be a part of it; you think about how it took so much extra work for them to do something new and how proud you are of them; you think about the one child who has a vitally important doctor's appointment tomorrow – you hope it goes well; you research different ways to help, or reach out in social media communities to try and find solutions to situations. Ultimately, you're committed to finding something new to make a difference – not for you, but for him, for her, for them. I really could write forever.

I want you to know that I constantly aim to understand what you're going through: I know that you face such incredible difficulties, all of which are entirely out of your control. My greatest hope is to help you, your children, and your family. So, if writing this book can make a meaningful difference in just one life, it will have been worth it.

As we move to the beginning of this book – I hope this is start of a journey that will change your life and your family's forever – I'd like to share a story I keep close to my heart. You may have heard it before, but it's worth repeating. Working with special needs families, yet never truly experiencing what it is like to walk in your shoes, this story has given me a rich understanding of your perspective and has, for me, framed your situation poignantly. Emily Perl Kingsley writes:

"When you're going to have a baby, it's like planning a fabulous vacation trip – to Italy. You buy a bunch of guide books and make your wonderful plans. The Colosseum. The Michelangelo David. The gondolas in Venice. You learn some handy phrases in Italian. It's all very exciting.

After months of eager anticipation, the day finally arrives. You pack your bags and off you go. Several hours later, the plane lands. The stewardess comes in and says, "Welcome to Holland."

"Holland?!?" you say. "What do you mean Holland?? I signed up for Italy! I'm supposed to be in Italy. All of my life I've dreamed of going to Italy."

But there's been a change in the flight plan. They've landed in Holland and there you must stay.

The important thing is that they haven't taken you to a horrible, disgusting, filthy place, full of pestilence, famine, and disease. It's just a different place.

So you must go out and buy new guide books. And you must learn a whole new language. And you will meet a whole new group of people you would never have met.

It's just a different place. It's slower paced than Italy, less flashy than Italy. But after you've been there for a while and you catch your breath, you look around…and you begin to notice that Holland has windmills…and Holland has tulips. Holland even has Rembrandts.

But everyone you know is busy coming and going from Italy and they're all bragging about what a wonderful time they had there. And for the rest of your life, you will say "Yes, that's where I was supposed to go. That's what I had planned."

And the pain of that will never, ever, ever go away…because the loss of that dream is a very significant loss.

But, if you spend your life mourning the fact that you didn't get to go to Italy, you may never be free to enjoy the very special, the very lovely things about Holland."

Breaking Through Special Needs

Here is my wish for you: I hope that by the end of this book I will have helped clarify some things for you and that you, just for a moment, will be reminded that you are doing an *exceptional* job.

Being an Advocate

"Every child deserves a champion: an adult who will never give up on them, who understands the power of connection and insists they become the best they can possibly be." - Rita Pierson

I'd like to start this book here; this is the place where every special needs parent has stood and felt overwhelmed. We need to talk about how you can be an advocate for your child in the face of what may seem like insurmountable obstacles. Let this chapter be a support for you.

It's likely that, if you have an older child and have navigated "the system" long enough, there may not be much to say that you haven't already experienced. In that case, it may be that this section is primarily geared towards the parents of special needs children who are just starting out on their journeys and are navigating everything for the first time. As you read this, you may one of the parents who are maybe afraid to "step on any toes", or perhaps you are concerned about your decision affecting someone's feelings even though it's likely in the best interest of your child. Whoever you are, whether you've gone through it all and have an older child, or whether you're at the beginning of your road with a younger son or daughter, I'd like you to keep reading. You may get insight into things you never knew.

If your child is older, then, it's possible that you've already had your fair share of experiences with insurance not approving equipment, for example, or applying for Medicaid services to no avail. The mountains of paperwork you're expected to fill out at every single doctor's appointment can seem overwhelming and deflating at the best of times: neurology, orthopedics, podiatry, pediatric ophthalmology... sigh. Did I summaries that well? And of course, that's all without mentioning the teachers, therapists, nurses, and aides that you also need to communicate with on a daily basis. If I'm honest, it would be surprising if you didn't feel a bit like a deer in the headlights at this point.

Yet you know, and I know, that these children – your child – don't always have voices. They need you to scale the mountains of paperwork, to fill in the forms, to maintain a lifestyle superwoman/superman would only dream of. They aren't always able to speak-up for themselves in distressing situations, or tell you when something is wrong. They are so innocently themselves – and that's so much of why we love them unconditionally. Your child requires parents, caregivers, therapists – THE WHOLE TEAM – to be his/her advocates. You are his/her voice.

Here's the truth, though: all too often parents think that all the responsibility falls directly on their shoulders. I want you to remember that you can reach out for support or ask your team for their opinions on the next steps in hard situations. So many of the parents I work with on a daily basis say that "it takes a village," yet they are often left wondering how they've ended up being the ones doing everything. I know that making the decisions you make – *the hard decisions* – can exhaust you, but you don't need to do this on your own. Even if your child is verbal and can communicate, they often need you to be the leader – so, let your team help support you in your role to guide the child you love. .

Your plates are full.

So full, in fact, that it's often hard to take a step back and assess whether you're still standing on your own two feet. I know it's not easy for you.

I'd like to share a few stories from my past... you may even catch a glimmer of yourself in them as you read along.

Earlier in my career, I was working with a little girl, aged 4, in my office. I'd gotten to know her mom well, and we were talking about her daughter's other therapies and programs, how school was that day... the usual. She started telling me that she had observed a session her daughter had with the school PT. She explained that the therapist barely did anything and that her daughter was only mildly engaged in the session. Before we continue, I'd like to tell you, right now, that not every therapist or teacher will be the best for your child. At the end of the day, *you* know your child best, regardless of anyone else's opinions.

As the mother talks, I asked her why she felt that way, that is, why she felt the therapist "barely did anything" with her daughter. She explained

Breaking Through Special Needs

that she felt the school therapist wasn't a good fit – she wasn't challenging or helping her daughter do her best. If this had been an isolated incident, I would likely have said everyone has "off" days from time to time, and that she should just keep an eye on what they are working towards and check in again soon. In this case, however, the child's mother had raised several consecutive concerns regarding the same school therapist.

Now, I would never discredit any other therapist. What I will say is that there are *good* and *bad* in any profession. Of course, it's very subjective and we should keep that in mind. Also – every child is different: different kids mesh well with different types of people. In the same way that you choose your friends, your child bonds with their therapist or anyone who works closely with them. Hence, getting the right fit is crucial!

As we continued to chat, I asked the child's mother whether she had discussed her child's goals with the school therapist. Challenge #1 surfaced. She couldn't. **The beautiful thing about school therapies is that children are able to receive necessary services in their school setting. The downfall of school therapies is, however, that according to the governing law, all goals MUST be so that the children can be the best versions of themselves in ONLY the school setting.**

Hmmm, what does that mean? Well, as it stands, all school-based goals MUST be related to the school environment. That is to say, the individual situation of the child gets lost in translation. No stairs in school, but stairs at home? Oh well. Guess they don't need to learn how to do stairs. They're in a chair most of the day? Oh well. Learning to independently crawl won't be relative for them in the school setting. Despite the very best intentions of a school based therapist, they cannot veer from protocol and therefore it further limits what they can do for the communities they serve, not to mention the lack of funding so they can have the equipment they need.

As a consequence, school therapists don't typically ask what goals the parent has for their child. They don't have the opportunity to sit down with them and see what is most important and work towards that. Often, if it isn't valued by the agency or school that is providing the services, they don't even get the time to be able to speak with them thoroughly.

Breaking Through Special Needs

Communication is sadly limited, and schools and agencies think that a short note in a communication notebook is sufficient enough The problem is, the child's progress is stunted by the fact that the therapist and the parents just aren't on the same page. Both parties have to work together in order to foster progress. I have come to understand this from personal experience, having worked in a school setting and feeling incredibly limited as to what I could do to help the kids I was working with. I knew that, despite my very best intentions, I wasn't providing the best opportunity for the kids I was helping and it forced me to make a drastic change.

Don't hesitate to reach out to the therapists or teachers in school. Tell them what you really want for your child.

Sure, you might feel a little uneasy the first time you do it, but how is anyone going to know what you want for your child if you don't communicate effectively with them? If you want your child to work towards crawling by themselves, then make it known. If you want him/her to start using a communication device or sign language, make it known. The therapists in the school WILL listen and will try to do the best they can to incorporate these goals into the school setting. I promise. You have to realize that they'll never know what you want if you don't tell them. Try a simple "let's set up a time to talk" conversation – I bet you'll be happily surprised at the results.
At the end of the day, the mother in my office felt as though her daughter wasn't being effectively challenged. Maybe the school therapist wasn't working towards the goals that this mother saw for her child. I decided that we should discuss the next steps. Did she think she should have a discussion with this therapist about her child's goals? Did she want to request changing the therapist at school?

Ultimately, the discussion led to the child's mother telling me that she didn't think the school therapist was bad, but that she wanted more for her daughter. At the end of the day, she simply felt as though the school therapist couldn't give her daughter what she needed. After listening, I explained that I understood and I suggested she request a change of therapist at school. She immediately became nervous and explained that she didn't know who to talk to about it, and that she would feel guilty if the therapist was swapped; she didn't want to hurt the therapist's feelings. This is human nature and I immediately understood why she felt that way. Of course you don't know who to talk about it because you typically have to trial and error and figure things out on your own as you navigate this new world.

I often find these emotions are relative to all parents of younger special needs children – sometimes older, too. It's part of the role you've been given. Overcoming the feeling that "you can't step on any toes" to get what you need for your child is something I'm sure you've already experienced. And yet, as hard and uncomfortable as it may be for you, you need to remember that you're your child's advocate. Flip the script and think about how much you love your child and will do anything for them. I'm not saying become the hulk… I'm just nudging you towards being the strong, authoritative voice of your child – the one he/she needs you to be. This goes for ANY parent, but especially parents of a child who doesn't have his/her own voice and isn't able to advocate for themselves.

At the end of the day, the mother requested a switch and was resultantly paired with a therapist much better suited to her daughter's needs. This is a positive result she may have not experienced if she hadn't overcome the fear of upset or guilt; she decided what was best for her daughter and had the courage of her conviction. I'm still so proud of her.

Let me share another story with you.

Here at *Breakthrough PT*, we currently see a client who is able to walk, but really lacks the balance and coordination to do it safely; he always needs help and his hand held. I received an email from his mom looking for some validation. She explained that her son's aide in school had been allowing him to use his stroller to get around. Sure, a stroller was "easier", but was it really encouraging him to be independent? I could tell she was upset. The more her son got used to the stroller, the more he'd request it and depended on it. *She was reasonably upset and taken back by this.* She just didn't understand why they'd allow him to sit all day… in an emergency – of course – but, for day-to-day activities she just couldn't understand why.

Here's the thing. As a parent, you obviously don't know what goes on in the day-to-day activities at school or in adult programs. You can hope that your child is safe and effectively challenged, but without having a live

Breaking Through Special Needs

footage camera, there's just no way of knowing. This scenario requires you to relinquish control over the situation. I know this is the case, because I've heard from parents just how scary that can be.

In this situation, Mom came up with a viable solution after we talked. I suggested that she contact the school to discuss the situation and what she really wanted for her son. She explained to the school that it's okay if it takes him longer to get somewhere, but that she just wants him to do it to the best of his ability. She needed to tell them that she did not want him to be wheeled around just for time's sake. Luckily, after that conversation, the situation drastically improved.

Encouraging you to be an advocate is about making your child's voice heard through you. Now, that isn't to say that you need to explode or have no patience: I just want to encourage you to look at it from your child's perspective. Ask yourself, "can I live with this situation?", and "is it in the best interest of my child, myself, and my family?" Let that be your guiding light and take decisive action accordingly.

These situations are going to come up all of the darn time. There are going to be instances when you're unhappy with the way something is being carried out, or you don't feel as though your child is being challenged enough. Unfortunately, there's no avoiding it. And, let's be honest – this doesn't only happen to special needs parents... it happens to everyone.

As humans – not just special needs parents – we often feel responsible for other people's feeling. We suppress our own in the face of them. In fact, we often don't want to be "that person"; we want to be on everyone's good side. These feelings are exacerbated when you're the parents of a special needs child: you're advocating for someone who can't fight his/her own battles and who possibly can't speak and/or fight for himself/herself. You therefore HAVE TO speak out – and the anxiety and nervousness can be overwhelming. I do, however, encourage you to be brave for your child and make the right decisions. Lean on your support system and take courage from the fact that you're doing the right thing.

Next time you find that you're unhappy with something, but you don't want to speak up, ask yourself: "why do I not want to change the situation?" Is it because you understand people make mistakes and it's the first time something has happened? Or, is it because you are afraid to hurt someone's feelings and be 'that person'? Make the decision to act accordingly.

FIND THE RIGHT PEOPLE FOR YOUR CHILD'S CARE

This might be the most important part of this book. Scratch that – this IS the most important part of this book. Find the most important people for your child's care. If you only take one thing away from my book at the end of it... please make it this. Let's unpack this concept – we'll do it from my perspective as a business owner first, and then we'll relate it back to you. Ready? Let's go.

I started a business having no clue what I was doing; I just knew (and still know) that I wanted to serve this community. I had big, grand plans for everything I wanted to provide for families with special needs children. I worked hard to achieve them, and to this day my dreams get bigger. As I worked towards my goals early on in my career, though, my baby business started to grow and I suddenly needed people on my team to help me continue to help more families. I wanted to expand! So, I hired some people that fit perfectly... and also some people that didn't fit perfectly.

Ultimately, what it came down to was *values*. Did the members on my team share the values of our mission and our business? I found that some did, and some didn't – and dealing with the repercussions meant that there were hard decisions I had to make. Finding people to trust in this business – people I trust to take care of the families that I feel are my own – feels like a daunting task. Why? Because it is. It's hard finding people that share the same values you do AND who you can trust. Here's the thing, though, it is not impossible.

In your situation, then, you have a revolving door. What does that mean? Well, there are people you *must* interact with for your child's care – some will be good, other's less so; some will come and stay, others will leave. It's up to you to make those critical decisions. We all know you've walked into a doctor's office and been outraged by the way they treated you and your child. I've heard parents relay incidents by saying: "They didn't even touch my son"; "They didn't even spend five minutes with me."; "They didn't listen to what I was trying to tell them."; "They just shrugged it off

like it was nothing."; "They just told me not to worry."; "I'm not even sure what the next step is."; "They just told me they could do surgery."; "They told me she needs Botox, what do I do?". This can be so incredibly debilitating – so, you have to ask yourself, are these the people I
want in my child's life?

I've heard even more disturbing things: "They told me she's not cognitive."; "They told me he'd never walk."; "They told me and my parents I'd never speak."; "They told me there's no point because she won't be able to do it by herself anyway."; "They told me he'd only get worse." I know – it's heartbreaking.

If this sounds familiar, you're not alone.

Unfortunately, these types of responses are relayed to me all too often. The worst part of it is that I've heard something like this from *every single one of my parents*. How is that possible and why in the world is this happening? In reality, what this comes down to – aside from, of course, ignorance – is a lack of shared values. Unfortunately, doctors do not always share your values – please understand that. They will not always subscribe to your goals and commitment. It's a sad reality, but it is true. Just remember, when it comes to doctors, though location may limit your choice, you do have the choice as to how you receive the information you are given.

This is a very powerful concept.

I guarantee that – simply because you've taken the time to sit down and read this book – that you are certainly the type of parent that goes above-and-beyond to ensure that you are doing everything and anything possible for your child. I'm really proud of you – it takes courage to do what you're doing. You're the parent who wants your child to be the best version of themselves so that they can be as independent as possible – and you will stop at nothing to make sure that happens. For this reason, I know that when you're failed by doctors, specialists, and therapists, your heart sinks.

It's not fair.

Breaking Through Special Needs

No, it's not fair. You're right. It's completely and utterly ridiculous that someone could ever say some of the despicable things listed above - they don't even know your child, nor do they knows the lengths you're going to in order to give him/her the best life possible. What you need to understand, though, is that some people in the healthcare realm were trained very single-mindedly. They do not – and cannot – share your values. So, when you let go of your anger towards these people, you can start making the decisions that matter and make a change.

This is a good thing though, right? They can see the potential downside of things and they just want to be honest with you about that. They view the world with what limitations there are... versus possibilities. They view the world in the lens they learned from school: diagnoses, problems, limitations, restrictions, possible surgeries, etc. The thing about this is, though, that you don't. You're a parent that views the opportunities for your child. You view all of the possibilities there are for his/her to grow, learn, and be more independent. You view the world for your child in a way that they don't.

I'd like to now share a story that relates to this issue. It happened fairly recently and I think it underscores much of what I've been talking about.

Thanks to ever popular social media platforms, I've joined amazing groups for pediatric physical therapists: we can collaborate, ask questions, and learn from one another in an unprecedented way. Sounds great, right? I love being able to connect with others who share the same mindset in wanting to help this community. What's better than having a support group from around the world when you face something you're not sure how to deal with? I often feel very blessed to be part of these singular online communities.

During one particular instance, a newly qualified physical therapist asked a question in one of the groups I socialize in. She is a school physical therapist and mentioned that she was speaking with her client's parents. She explained that they just want their little boy to be able to ride a bike. She was looking for help on how to make a school goal orientated with this goal in mind, though she needed to mesh it with "the school environment".

Breaking Through Special Needs

There are a number of issues, here. For one thing, schools have many limitations as to "the school environment", particularly when it comes to structuring goals around it. If it doesn't relate to school, then it shouldn't technically be a goal. Understandably, therefore, many therapists in the group began to comment quite negatively. I must admit, I lost my temper at this point. Comments from therapists included "that's a P.E goal, not therapy, you shouldn't do that", "no, bike riding can't be worked on in school", "no, it's not possible", and "they don't have to ride a bike at school, so it shouldn't be a goal". I was livid. I should be fair in saying that there were a few therapists in there who tried to help, but the vast majority seemed to undermine the positive intentions of the young therapist by discounting her ideas outright – most comments vehemently stated that the goals of the school and those of the parents cannot harmoniously connect.

Honestly, this made my blood boil. Why were so many people in my profession saying *no*? I could not wrap my head around the fact that they would view it this way. Why is it that the school cannot listen to the parents' goals for their child? Why is it that we need to follow the terms and guidelines of what the school says is right for a special needs child while the parents' opinions are sidelined? Why would *the only opti*on be that we need to refer out to a different program? The school administrators are not qualified physical therapists. They don't know or understand the necessity of certain programs, goals, or modifications that need to be made – they will never, ever understand unless our community and the parents make them aware.

Enough is enough – we need therapists who put the parent's goals as the highest priority. Regardless of what "rules" there are, there is ALWAYS a way to relate parental goals back to the school setting. All parents want is for their child to be his/her best self and to be able to do as much as he/she possibly can.

Now, I can't change these therapists' points of view no matter how hard I try or as much as I want to. It is up to this profession to try and fight for you in every way we possibly can, but there will always be outliers in every field. I can tell you, however, that if you have a therapist on your team who does not take what you say as meaningful and vitally important, who doesn't fight for you in every single way possible, or who you feel doesn't have you and your child's best interests at heart… FIND

Breaking Through Special Needs

ANOTHER ONE. Go find someone who will listen, who will fight, and who will help you on your journey. We are out there – do not settle for a 'no'.

Doctors will often tell you of all the limits your child faces... the seriousness of scoliosis or that your child will never talk or walk, or that they are only "satisfactory" in meeting their IEP goals. But, you listen to me: they are used to seeing limitations... you aren't. Fight for your child.

Find a team of people that view the possibilities, not the limitations. Find a team that shares your values, your goals, and your commitment. Find a team that sees the potential to overcome the limitations your child is faced with and which other professionals have placed on them. These are the people you need.

You will be an advocate for your entire lifetime. Embrace the discomfort and find your own voice.

SPEAKING TO THOSE INVOLVED IN YOUR CHILD'S CARE

If my guess is right, you have a laundry list of people involved in your child's care. It takes a village, right?

Nurses, aides, teachers, teachers' aides, physical therapists, occupational therapists, speech therapists, vision therapists, behavioral therapists, counselors, orthoptists... then there are the doctors such as neurologists, orthopedics, pediatricians, physiatrists, and every other specialist out there. I'm sure I'm not even covering 50% of it for some of you!

At some point you've probably asked yourself: "what *should* the communication look like?" When referencing the school system, oftentimes a notebook is passed back and forth between the teachers, aides, nurses, and therapists. It's then sent home for the parent to read. At this point, the parents respond via the notebook (sometimes) and the teacher will see them at the next parent/teacher conference. Now, this is okay... it's not as if every detail of every single day needs to be written down and documented for you. However, it is important to know the big details. You'll often get reports on things such as what they ate that day, what happened in therapy, what they did as a class, etc. Sometimes little really changes from day to day, but if it's a trend that you're getting the same old report for the third week in a row, and there have been no changes in therapy or otherwise, then that's a problem.

I know firsthand that small changes are made from session to session. While school therapies are limited in their time- frame, their status often changes from week to week. For example, if I am treating one of my clients with Spastic Quadriplegic Cerebral Palsy, they might use a lot of extensor tone one day with difficulty controlling movements, and the next time I see them they may be a tired and have difficulty holding themselves up using their tone. Their status changes daily and their therapists should be noting those changes. While they may not be significant differences, if they are including small changes in their reports to you, that means they are paying attention.

It's so often that parents come to me frustrated and venting about how they have no clue what's going on in their child's school therapy. I've even had parents telling me that they don't really know what's going on with their children at school. And that's okay! Everyone is different, but you need to make sure they are giving you information that is enough for you *personally*. Sometimes, parents don't need or want to know all the details, and sometimes parents need to know ALL of the details. Regardless of which type of parent you are, it's important to communicate with the school effectively so as to make sure you're receiving what's enough for you. If you ask for more – that's okay. You're not wrong for asking for more details, or for calling them to see what's been going on lately. You have every right to know. If you don't need as much, that's okay too. You just need to know what's right for *you*. To elaborate, if you aren't getting enough information, then you have to speak up. Whether you'd like them to write more frequently in the notebooks, or you'd like to schedule a visit to sit in on their therapy session – it is all within your rights.

This doesn't just apply to school based visits; it's just harder in that scenario because you don't attend school with your child. Take this example, for instance: in my outpatient facility, we had a new client that signed up for one of our programs. She comes weekly – for one hour – to work towards her goals. Her mother had initially brought her daughter in for an evaluation and one or two treatment sessions. Following one of her child's sessions, she called us to open up and tell us that her daughter needs a little more out of us. She felt that her daughter is the type of girl that loves a lot of energy in her sessions – no loud cheering, though – and that we should make everything into a game or else she just feels as though she's doing work and won't want to continue coming back. Of course we were receptive – in fact, we were appreciative, as we want to do everything we can to help our clients. Our therapist later called her back to discuss the details and then immediately changed the energy in the next session. We were immediately tremendously grateful that this mom had opened up to us about what she was feeling. It often takes time for therapists to learn about each child and what works for them, and it can take a few sessions to work that out. This mom understood, but was also helping facilitate building the relationship with her daughter so that she would get the most out of coming to our facility.

We told her how grateful we were that she felt comfortable enough to tell us her concerns and thoughts before they became an issue and inhibited her daughter's progress. This mom was the perfect example of an advocate for her daughter; she communicated clearly and effectively so that we could make the changes her daughter needed. Be aware that not every parent feels comfortable doing this, and not every therapist or doctor creates an environment where this is accepted. Please don't let this stop you, though. This mother's daughter is now getting more benefit from each session. Why? Well, the simple act of communicating with us to help us guide her daughter made all the difference. After all, she knows her daughter the best.

If you don't have professionals in your life who allow you to speak up without getting defensive, then you have the wrong team members. The right providers will love how involved you want to be rather than seeing it as a threat. The same principle goes for communicating, scheduling visits for school therapies, asking about goals and why they're working on certain things, and whatever else you can think of. Don't be afraid to take a stance and get involved.

COLLABORATION OF CARE

Alongside making sure you're speaking to those involved in your child's care, it's also important that those healthcare professionals are collaborating *together* in order to work towards the goals you have for your child. Every situation is different, but you typically have multiple health professionals on your child's team. Because my office is an outpatient

Breaking Through Special Needs

one, for example, my clients receive home and school services. This means they could have up to three different physical therapists. If all three therapists don't work together towards the ultimate goals of the family, then it creates a huge detriment to the client's progression.

In lieu of this, we've often spoken to other therapists in coordination of a child's care, and they have discussed how they've only been working on specific areas. If that's the case, and the child needs more repetitions, or we can complement that activity, we do so. We wouldn't know to do this unless we spoke with them. Too often, I've tried contacting a school or home therapist who is not receptive to collaborating or, worse still, becomes defensive. This does not help the client at all! Sometimes, I've even mentioned what's worked for me and have been shrugged off because they are unwilling to be open to change or suggestion. Luckily, that isn't always the case; we've spoken with plenty of other professionals on collaboration of care for individual clients. We, too, find people who share our values.

The most important part of this chapter is that you need to have people on your team who are willing to do what needs to be done and who share your values. Find the therapists who are willing to work with you in order to make your child's life the best it can possibly be – don't be afraid to challenge, share your views, and get involved. Be the advocate you've been tasked to be!

Isolation Is Real

Being an advocate for your child can be tough, but not only that… it can be pretty lonely. No one will ever really understand what the type of isolation you experience at times truly feels like. I've talked to so many parents who share similar feelings of loneliness and sadness at times. Anxiety, depression, grief … all of these are incredibly challenging to deal with, and usually they aren't isolated emotional states. Things happen all the time… altogether. You can't help but experience heart-ache when you feel like the following parents: "My child isn't asked on play dates."; "I don't really relate to my family or friends."; "It's hard to have a conversation with people"; "Nobody really understands what it takes to just get out of the house"; "I usually have to cancel plans last minute if [my child] isn't having a good day". And those are just a few of the repeated statements I've heard, so I'm sure you've gad to grapple with these situations and more on a daily basis.

These instances, especially because of their frequency, can make you feel like you're in this alone. Most commonly, all of your efforts and attention is focused on your family, specifically your special needs child. You try to pull everything together for everyone else, yet have failed to recognize your own needs, haven't you? You've probably not stopped and thought, am I alright?

Now, I am not writing this to pass ANY judgement – I've never walked in your shoes and can't begin to decipher how you're feeling. But, I *can* tell you what I see every day here at my clinic Breakthrough PT. I constantly talk to parents just like you in my clinic. So, what I'd really like to talk to you about, here, is that if you don't take care of yourself, you cannot give the best care to your child or your family. You see, your *best self* is usually battered down by stress and work, keeping up with appointments, and running around trying to remember to get groceries; you also have worry when your child isn't meeting milestones, or that they need a change in seizure meds, for example, or that they're demonstrating a new and different behavior that you've never seen. There is so much going on – you need to take stock.

Breaking Through Special Needs

It's the worry that catches up to you.

Please understand that you can only keep juggling 20 balls in the air for so long until they all start crashing down. Even if you think you can outlast the stress... something has got to give. Some of you are doing this without a spouse, nurses, or aides. But, that does NOT mean you're alone... even if it feels like it.

I was speaking to one mom recently; we were just discussing a weekend birthday party they had attended. She was telling me that her son was FINALLY invited to a birthday party and that he finally felt well enough to go to it and risk the exposure to germs. All of the other kids were playing in the bouncy-castle and running up and down the slides. For this mom, she faced a very hard choice. All of the other parents at this party had kids that could run and play freely while they chatted about the latest school drama, but her son... her son wasn't capable of doing those things. I remember her getting misty eyed as she said:

> "He couldn't run like they could. He couldn't play and run up and down the slides, but he still had the biggest smile on his face just being there. Yet all I could feel was so much sadness because I was sitting by the other parents and he couldn't interact with the other kids – I felt guilty. I went over and tried to help him participate, but it was so dangerous with everyone running around that I just packed my things up and said we had somewhere else we needed to be before I started crying."

Even writing that is saddening. Have you ever felt something similar? Have you ever felt resentful at the fact that you needed to make this kind of choice, but that the other parents didn't. Have you felt that it wasn't fair? This mom felt a complex mix of emotions that she felt no-one would ever understand. She felt lonely.

As an added component, even with as many technological advancements as there are nowadays, the accessibility of all places is still extremely limited. This can also take its toll on you, though not many people understand that. The thing is, oftentimes people don't fully comprehend the limitations until they're put in specific situations.

Breaking Through Special Needs

I can't tell you how many times I've traveled on the Long Island Rail Road to Penn Station in NYC, or to JFK International Airport via public transportation – I take this type of travel for granted at times. For one of my client's parents, however, it was a completely different story on one of their journeys. They went to see *Frozen* in the city, and to take the stress off, they decided not to drive and to take the railroad to Penn Station instead. They ended up having to carry their 12 year old daughter in her wheelchair up and down flights of steps because there was no working elevator where they were. How can this be? They also had to walk several blocks more just to get to an accessible form of transportation. I was shocked. Until I heard this story it hadn't even crossed my mind as to the issues they might face on such a routine journey – one I often take! I then started recognizing all of the places that lacked accessibility, and a bigger issue started to become clear.

A powerful phrase a parent once said to me after a challenging family trip was this: *"It's like the world doesn't even want you in it… like they're trying to keep you out of the places that everyone else is in. It's so frustrating."*

So now, not only are you concerned that your child is well enough or is having a good enough day when you venture out, but you also constantly consider noise levels, if your child with sensory concerns can handle it, if there are adequate bathroom facilities and changing tables for older children, or if there is wheelchair accessibility. Ultimately, for you, it's just easier to stay home. I completely understand that. Even going to family members homes' is difficult if they don't have accessible entrances. It's truly so hard.

In addition, when all is said and done, your lives end up revolving around doctor's visits, therapies, and procedures, while everyone else you know is with their children on travel sports teams or family vacations. You are living a completely different lifestyle which nobody really understands. Some parents are even unable to work outside of the home and maintain a job; they need to care for their special needs child.

More isolation.

I am speaking from the vantage point of a physical therapist working so closely with families like yours every single day, and I am in no way a psychologist….however, I *am* someone who genuinely cares about your wellbeing and that of your child. Something we do every day at our clinic when working with families and speaking with parents is to encourage self-care as much as possible. *We want you to be the healthiest, happiest you so that you child can be the healthiest, happiest him/her, too.*

So, in order to get you smiling, I've compiled a list of some self-care tips you can start working through, right now. They're simple, can be worked into your daily routine, and can be life-changing:

1. Take a deep breath before getting up in the morning.
2. Go for a 5 minute walk outside in the fresh air.
3. Light your favorite smelling candle.
4. Read a few chapters in your favorite book.
5. Make a peaceful playlist to listen to in the car.
6. Write something you're grateful for each morning.
7. Print and frame a few pictures that make you smile.
8. Go to bed early.

And though these are only a few ideas, and some of them may not even be reasonably attainable for you in your current situation, I challenge you to find something that *is*.

In fact, you might be able to find a local support group. We frequently host *Facebook Live* parent support presentations and workshops or webinars. Why? Because we KNOW how hard it is getting out of the house – *Facebook Live* or *Zoom* lets you watch a replay at any time that's convenient for you. I encourage you to find something similar in your area, or join ours by following @Breakthrough Intensive Physical Therapy on *Facebook*. There is help in the community, just allow yourself to find it. **Make it a promise to yourself that you will not lose hope**. You're so used to making promises and keeping commitments to everyone else but yourself, so the time has come to take a step back and recompose.

I can hear some of you sighing and whispering under your breath: "But, I feel guilty taking any time for myself". Here's the thing, though, you spend endless hours caring for your child – making sure they have the best of EVERYTHING – so, you should never, not for a single second,

Breaking Through Special Needs

feel guilty for taking some time for yourself. If you don't do this, then you won't be able to be the best for your child.

I'm being very honest when I say that you make seriously busy people look like they are on vacation. The stress you deal with is no-doubt overwhelming at times. You've probably researched methods of reducing stress before, but most likely haven't found time for that either. The truth is, stress will wear your body down over time. Stress hormones circulate in your body constantly, thereby causing physiologic changes that can affect your overall health. And if you're affected, what would happen to you child?

Chronic stress can:

1. Raise your blood pressure.
2. Increase your risk of heart attack or stroke.
3. Increase your risk for Diabetes type II.
4. Cause heartburn or acid reflux.
5. Cause digestive issues including nausea and constipation.
6. Cause headaches or body aches.
7. Lower your immune system.

These are just a few of the negative effects of chronic stress and they shouldn't be taken lightly.

Now, you may already be thinking: "Didn't't she just say she knows we have no time for self-care or ANYTHING, and now she's asking us to try and incorporate more things into our day!?" If I were you, I would probably be thinking that, too. BUT… it's important to note that, if you ignore your health and are unable to balance or manage your stress, your loved ones will suffer too. I am asking you to make time, because if you don't, you'll lose even more.

Happily, I'm not going to leave you hanging and am here to help. I've put together just a few different methods that you may be willing to try in order to reduce your stress. These are simple and can be short in duration. If you don't already do any of these, I encourage you to try at least try ONE of them. Attempting even just one is definitely worth it. Why? Because spiraling down the stress tunnel will be never-ending and it will only result in other issues. Take a look and get de-stressing!

Breaking Through Special Needs

1. JOURNALING:

Have you ever thought of doing this? It only requires paper, a pen, and 5-10 minutes of your time. Try picking a time during your day when it is LEAST hectic (do your best). It may be in the morning, or it could be when everyone is asleep at night. Writing is powerful. It allows you to recognize your thoughts and feelings, thereby helping you release them onto paper. I know for me, personally, journaling helps me make better decisions and become more self-aware in what matters most. Journaling is a wonderful de-stressor.

2. MEDITATION:

Most of us have tried this, and if you haven't tried it before, then you're probably giggling at the idea of it now. Stay with me, though. It is definitely challenging, but with repetition it actually gets easier. To be honest, I laughed the first few times… but then, after MANY attempts at making it a habit, it has finally sort-of stuck. Meditation can be hard, but it can definitely help reduce stress and slow your thoughts down.

3. EXERCISE:

I don't mean get those shoes on and go run ten miles. I simply mean *move your body*. Go for a walk, have a dance party, perform a yoga routine, whatever it is that works and motivates you. I know it isn't for everyone, but if it's something you want to do and haven't gotten into yet, it is worth the try. This seems crazy, but exercise will actually increase your energy levels even if it is just for 30 minutes a day. Not only does this help you keep up with your crazy lifestyle, it will also help you sleep more soundly at night. A well-rested you means a less stressed you.

4. ATTENDING A SUPPORT GROUP:

You're probably thinking, "Com'on Christine, I don't have time for this". Hold your horses! There are many local in-person groups and online groups out there. Research what is available to you and try it out. We have seen it at our own support group: sometimes just sharing your story offers relief in-and-of itself. Other parents in the group will have a good understanding of your situation and will never judge you, and sometimes this can be the missing puzzle piece.

Breaking Through Special Needs

5. GRATITUDE:

This can be practiced in combination with any of the other things I've mentioned. You can write out a list of everything you are grateful for, or you can even just spend a few minutes thinking about them. There are actually scientific studies based on these thought processes: gratitude changes your mindset and your attitude, and it can also help you see what really matters in very stressful and hard times.

These are just a few of MANY things out there for you to try in order to reduce your stress. I challenge you to try at least ONE of them, and please do let us know how it works for you. Remember, it is not only you that suffers when you are overwhelmed with stress: your loved ones can, too. So, be sure to try and find the balance you are looking for. In case you want smaller, day-by-day ideas, I'm including a link you can use to sign up for our self-care calendar. I give this calendar to parents across the country in the hope that, even if they only follow it for a few days, it helps them navigate stressful moments. I hope it will help you, too, in reminding you to take just a minute or two for yourself. Print it out, hang it up, and USE it.

Head to our website at: www.breakthroughptli.com/resources and get your free resource, now!

PARENT REFLECTIONS

Throughout the years during which I've worked with special needs families, one thing has always remained constant: they are treated differently. I have heard countless stories of struggles parents face, but, fortunately, some really amazing stories, too. I recently had a conversation with the mother of a child I work with. We were talking about what it's like for her going out into the community. She was describing what sounded like such a hectic, scary, and frustrating day... but, this was her norm. When going out to a family event, shopping at the mall, or even on her average grocery trip, she experiences staring, mumbling, and "weird looks". I was angry at hearing this, but knew it must be incredibly difficult for her.

Breaking Through Special Needs

I know that it is different for all of you, but the reason I really wanted to talk about this is because we need to talk about what we can do to change things. Do we believe that people just don't know better? Do we think they just aren't sure how to react around a child or adult with special needs? Is it that they don't know how to communicate well? We need to figure this out.

So, in response to this discussion, I asked a group of parents the following: "If you could say anything to people about what it's like to parent a child with special needs, what would it be?"

These were the very powerful responses I received...

"What does it feel like—lonely, isolating...you feel like others judge your child as badly behaved, damaged, contagious – that they judge you as if your child is a product of your poor parenting. I could go on and on about how much preparation is required before an outing into the community. We don't just hop in the car and hit the mall or supermarket. What does it feel like? Exhausting."

"Admittedly, my response to this question might be different year-to-year, or even day-to-day, but today... Do not feel sorry for us. We are the lucky ones."

"I am just like you. I am not a superhero for being a special needs mom and coping with all that comes with it. You would do the same if it were your child. But, if you do happen to see me looking a wreck, rushed, flustered, overwhelmed, etc... ya know what? A smile goes a long way. Hold the door open for me. Ask me what I think of the weather lately. I need a little more typical in my life. Just please... don't stare. My child and I are not a freak show. We do not want to be observed or judged. And don't feel sorry for me... I don't need it. My daughter has made me strong. In the end we all want acceptance. I want acceptance for my child. However, if crossed I will bring out Mamma Bear and you will be sorry you ever woke up that morning."

"Please don't ignore my child. Talk to her and treat her like you would any other child."

"Don't for a moment believe that you know my experiences, or the experiences of any other special needs family, no matter who you know. First, just like any other child, my child is unique. Would you presume to understand all there is to know about a child you just met simply by knowing their age and gender? If you've met one child with autism, you have met one child with autism. If you are interested in what it's like to

Breaking Through Special Needs

live in my shoes, ask me in a kind and respectful way and at an appropriate time. I assure you, you will not know what it's like otherwise."

"Don't presume that caring for my child makes me super mom. Taking care of my kids doesn't make me a great mom, it just makes me a mom – that's what we do."

"It is the most challenging, yet rewarding thing I could ever do. It is the most challenging because there is a constant state of grieving for the child you still have, but not the one you expected, yet you still need to be able to cope and care for your medically complex child. I grieve the milestones my daughter will never reach, but other girls her age will. It's something I try not to think about until I see the little girls dressed as ballerinas heading to dance class."

"It is so rewarding because there is no purer form of love that I will receive but from my special needs child. She is an Angel sent to me. She has made me stronger and I bear the responsibility of 2 voices. My own and hers. I am her biggest cheerleader and her biggest advocate. Her milestones, no matter how small, are celebrated as if she was just accepted into Harvard, because I know it was that difficult for her to achieve. She is amazing and I know she changes lives. She changed mine."

I've been privileged to get to know all these parents and children a little better; I've seen the ups and downs of parenting a special needs child. I know that some days are better than others, but one thing stands true… you grow from each and every experience you encounter. Whenever there's a new experience that's extremely tough, you make it out on the other side and are stronger and smarter because of it. I know you learn from the good moments, too.

At my clinic, *Breakthrough Intensive PT*, we asked parents the following, also: "What would you tell your one year ago self?" We wanted to compile a series of answers so that we could/can reflect on all of the amazing, hard, sad, happy, frustrating, and grateful experiences they've had in their journeys. We received some beautiful responses:

"Relax, you're in the thick of it. Just breathe."

"Don't second guess yourself. Don't blame yourself. Let go of the past."

Breaking Through Special Needs

"I am one person with two hands! I say this to myself over and over again…We as special needs parents cannot do it all! We are human and can only be in one place at a time!"

"I'm strong enough to deal with anything that comes my way!"

"One day at a time. One task at a time. Enjoy your special ones as much as you can despite our crazy schedules/therapies/ and doctor's appointments. And BREATHE! Everything works out in the end."

"Be strong. Pray to God that you get through one day at a time. It's not going to be easy. Sometimes you just have to take a deep breath, walk outside, come back in, and take care of your child."

"There's always somebody who has it a little harder than you. I'm grateful for what I have."

"Stay on top of those pulls and pains, stretch and get them checked out. As parents, we lift and lift and don't take care of ourselves and then the pain turns to more serious problems, which sometimes require surgery. So, stay on top of your own needs as well as everyone else's."

"The greatest challenge of being a special needs parent (or exceptional Mama, as I like to say) is actually extending the same patience and empathy to my neuro-typical child as I do to my son with Autism."

I'm guessing that you can relate to these in some shape or form. Self-care is so incredibly important for all of you – parents and caregivers alike; it's essential and a necessity.

Grief is a very real and present part of your journeys. It may fade or it may not, but you are constantly growing into a new phase of your life. You are constantly learning from your experiences and, no matter what you are thrown into, you come out stronger. As you reflect, I hope you allow yourselves the same patience you constantly give others. You are ALWAYS doing your best, and ultimately that is what matters.

I will never say that I know what it's like to walk in your shoes. I will only encourage you to be the best version of yourself for YOU first, but then also for your family. You are not alone – don't be afraid to seek help, whether that be from friends, family, or professionals.

Breaking Through Special Needs

Remember, you are doing an exceptional job. Take care of yourself – you are worth it.

Siblings Need Support Too

I've spoken about how important it is to look after yourself, to advocate for your special needs child, and to do the best for your family in the role you've been given. Now, then, I want to turn to your other children – all too often, the siblings of a special needs child seem to get left out of the predominant narratives, not at all because they are loved less, but simply because their brother/sister needs more time and attention. Having a child with special needs affects *all* members of the family. Routinely, support programs are offered to parents, but it is not typical to see support offered for the siblings. And this is a little heartbreaking. The repercussions of this are two-fold. On the one hand, the siblings lose out on vital attention from their parents, albeit unbeknownst to mom and dad, and furthermore, as siblings are most likely to spend the most time with the special needs child, it's sad when they don't know how/what to do. In fact, if you really think about it, siblings will likely spend the most time – and be in their lives the longest – out of anybody, including therapists, parents, and extended family members. Surely they need more support, then?

It wasn't until I was working in home care and was exposed to many different types of family dynamics and situations, that I saw how having children with special affected their siblings. In one particular case, I worked with a mother close to my heart; she has a little girl that I worked with and got to know well. She changed so much of my perspective, as she introduced me to a formal version of sibling workshops called *SibShops*. Interesting, right? I'd never heard of them before. Intrigued as I was, I ended up attending a two day conference with her; I enjoyed them so much and was able to learn how to host these myself to be the best benefit to these Sibs!

The first day of the conference focused on educating us about the siblings of special needs children. We were challenged to gain a deeper perspective on the unique *concerns* and *opportunities* they face during their lifetimes. Unique concerns included things such as embarrassment of their special needs sibling or experiencing a lack of attention from their parents. Having said that, these were just two amongst a very long list of

Breaking Through Special Needs

other issues. I was forced to be quite honest with myself: I hadn't realized that siblings experienced a vast majority of these feelings, though I had encountered multiple similarities in some of the families I worked with.

Although there was a long list of concerns, however, there was also an equally long list of unique opportunities these siblings have. This made me smile at the time, as it still does now. Learning how to be an advocate – especially at a young age – was included in the list. So was gaining access to resources, patience, and empathy. Isn't that wonderful?

Amongst the attendees in that workshop were healthcare professionals, service providers, adult siblings, and parents. It was inspiring to see the parents attending this workshop: they were there to gain insight into the struggles of their other children; they were trying to grow for *all of* their children. In fact, I felt as though I was the one growing: I gained such valuable perspectives, and though different, each one had unique and important value.

The second day was much more interactive. We all got to participate in an actual *SibShop* with children in the local area. While the day was filled with silly games and being goofy (not far off from my typical day, really! ☺), we witnessed the siblings opening up. Young children were discussing concerns and what they wished was different, but they were also speaking about what they enjoy about their brother or sister, as well as what makes them special. It's a beautiful thing to see.

If we look at all the benefits of a workshop such as this, I think it's important to explain what it really is. What are *SibShops* and why do parents and siblings need them so much?

Well, *SibShops* are "opportunities for brothers and sisters of children with special health and developmental needs to obtain support and education within a recreational context." (siblingsupport.org). They are not therapy groups, but rather present an opportunity for peer support; they allow siblings to feel less isolated and let them know that they are heard. It is a safe place for them to discuss what they like and dislike about having a sibling with special needs, while at the same time connecting with others who understand. It sounds amazing, right? And it is!

Breaking Through Special Needs

So, here's where you come in. I urge you to step into a sibling support workshop, even if your other children are supportive, are responsible, and are generally happy; it is so important to provide them with these opportunities, not only themselves, but also for your special needs child. These workshops can provide peer support, recreational fun, and mostly an opportunity to celebrate them as individuals and siblings of someone with special needs.

At *Breakthrough*, we host virtual *SibShops* each week in addition to our in-person workshops. This allows us to help siblings from everywhere and anywhere (we are nationwide!), and gives us the opportunity to provide resources that are not routinely available to them. Typically, they are hosted for ages 7-12, however, we have developed separate age categories to uniquely serve each age group based on what their unique experiences are at different points in development. If you haven't heard of one in your area, head to: **www.breakthroughptli.com/sibshop/** and sign up through that link – we'd love to meet you and your children.

Aside from the actual *SibShops* program itself, and/or finding a support program for your non-special needs children, there is a lot of value in *yourself* recognizing the concerns, worries, fears, frustrations, and joys that form part of having a sibling with special needs. There have been countless discussions in our workshops that have led to a greater depth and understanding of what your neuro-typical children truly go through on a day-to-day basis. And this type of knowledge can only help strengthen the bond with your children. Because I truly believe these SibShop-related revelations can be life-changing, I'm going to spend some time going through them with you, now.

What Challenges do They Face?

Some of their challenges are pretty obvious, even if you've only ever had your special needs child. These challenges help mold them into the incredibly caring and patient children they are. Even though they are obvious, that doesn't mean they are normal challenges that other children their age face, and they could even be things that you or I will never have to face. At our workshops, we've learned a tremendous amount from our siblings; I want to share what we've learned from them behind the scenes, all of which could help parents see some things more clearly. The following is compiled from observations and intake from our *Sibshops*:

Breaking Through Special Needs

Challenge #1: Friends Not "Getting It"

Boy, do we hear this during nearly every session! If you can think back to when you were younger – around your child's age – especially middle school where the start of teenage drama truly began, I bet you can remember it being a little bit of a challenge. It's a strange time when you're not really sure who you are yet, but you *are* certain of all of your insecurities: you choose to care a whole lot about things that won't matter ten years from now. Remember?

Well, finding a group of friends is hard enough at that age, so imagine having a sibling with special needs… it can make it really challenging to find *true friends*. Not only do siblings have the natural insecurities about themselves, but they have insecurities about their family, too. They try bringing friends over who don't understand why their sibling yells, hits, bites, doesn't talk, can't sit up by themselves, etc., and the list goes on and on. Understandably, they feel confused and more insecure than before. We've heard countless stories just about just this type of scenario. Here are some actual quotes from our siblings:

"I've tried bringing my friends over, but they get scared when my sister yells loudly and they only want to hang out at their house."

"I brought a friend over, but he didn't understand why my sister doesn't say anything. I tried explaining that she communicates differently, but he didn't really get it."

"One of my friends keeps making jokes that my sister follows us around all of the time; she doesn't want to hang out with her because she thinks she's 'weird'. I don't appreciate how she treats my sister."

"My brother doesn't really know how to manage things being different than what he wants, so then he gets mad and starts hitting me and my mom. He did that when a friend was over once and that friend never wanted to come back."

"I had a friend come over and all he could tell me about was how him and his brother were fighting over the remote. They both wanted to watch different things so they got in trouble because they kept grabbing

Breaking Through Special Needs

the remote out of each other's hands. I would do anything for my sister to grab the remote out of my hand. I wish that we fought over what to watch or that she would physically be able to do that."

Go ahead, grab your tissues…I'll wait here.

Sibling don't always find kids/friends that will be as understanding and accepting of differences as themselves. They are at a completely different level and are often more responsible and way more mature at their age than their peers. It causes a natural discrepancy in what they value and how they see the world. I'm certain that much of the lack of understanding in other children stems from a lack of exposure, of course. It is as also the fact that they may not know how to manage confusion. Sadly, at times it's also what they're taught from their parents and they aren't just "accepting" of others' differences.

When we look at siblings, we can see that they start valuing their relationships at an earlier age than probably you or I did. They value the few kids that will accept them and be their friend despite their siblings' differences. They especially value the friends who do "get it" – these are most often part of the *SibShops*. I always joke and say that at their age I was more concerned about what flavor ice cream I was going to have for dessert than the things that these kids worry about. And while it can get a laugh or two, it's actually true. In all honestly, I'm often in awe of their maturity and grace. These kids face so much more at a young age than their friends, and understandably this causes a natural disconnection from those they surround themselves with.

Challenge #2: What They Feel

Siblings of special needs children typically have a whole host of emotions that are not always understood or seen. Our workshops have been very enlightening and, as parents, you may not be aware of some of the following, daily feelings your children may experience:

Frustration

I can't tell you how many times we've heard how frustrating it is for siblings when they are held to a different set of standards than their special needs brothers/sisters. Yes, they realize their siblings can't help it sometimes, but they often get frustrated when, if their sibling does something such as get angry, hit, yell, etc., he/she doesn't receive the same punishment. In our workshops, they often express that their parents will yell at them for something, but if their sibling does it, the same punishment isn't dealt.

Neglect

When we do discussions, siblings will often express how they feel when their parents spend more time with their special needs brother/sister. Often, they express that their parents are so engaged with the needs of their sibling that they don't get the attention that they want from their parents. Usually, it's not necessarily the *physical* time spent with their sibling, rather, the issue lies with the emotional energy invested in one child which is restrained for the other.

Embarrassment

I'm sure you've already noticed this one: it's pretty hard to avoid. Perhaps you've even felt it, too, from time-to-time. The countless stories we've heard from siblings typically involve embarrassment. Whether going out to eat with their family and their sibling yells or throws, or people stare at their brother/sister, it all comes down to a daily struggle with embarrassment. Siblings are often insecure when their brother/sister does something that's "not socially acceptable" such as drooling, hitting, or being loud. Siblings in our workshops have even expressed embarrassment as an emotion that makes them want to avoid public places or outings with their families.

The Need To Be Perfect

If I had a single dollar for every competitive sibling of a special needs child I've met, that is, "perfectionists" in the making, then I would be writing this book from my yacht somewhere with much warmer weather. Jokes aside, siblings of special needs children are extremely special, but they place so much added stress on themselves. Why? Because everything they see you as a parent going through, they take on themselves. It may well be a form of compensation in an attempt to "make up" for their sibling's deficits in behavior or abilities, or it may even be even to avoid

Breaking Through Special Needs

adding extra stress on their parents' shoulders – either way, though, it is extremely prevalent amongst these siblings.

Fear

Fear typically comes up in every single workshop we run. It's a topic that, no matter what discussion we facilitate, becomes exposed. Sometimes it's fear about not fitting in with their friends; sometimes it's the fear of being alone; sometimes it's even the fear of what will happen as their sibling gets older. They'll often express these fears so eloquently – issues far beyond what their ages may suggest they deal with– and I, more often than not, marvel at the maturity of these children. They manage so much more than "typical" siblings will ever have to think about. In fact, I often think about their outlook in comparison to my own childhood: how different their reality is, and will always be, despite how much you, as a parent, try to keep "normalcy" as a part of their everyday lives.

When we talk about the future with them, they'll often start talking about how their sibling fits into that future. Isn't that incredible? The love these kids have for their siblings is beautiful. When we ask about what they dream of, or what they'd like their futures to look like, they'll say things such as, "I'll obviously have a side apartment so that [my sibling] can live with me and I can continue to take care of her when it's too hard for my parents". Wow. Sometimes we've even heard the following: "I don't know because I don't know what my family will be doing." It's the way their brains work. Amazingly, it's automatic: they think about their family and sibling before themselves. They'll even talk about the careers they'll choose directly in relation to their special needs brother/sister: most want, and do, serve others and go into careers that help those less fortunate. We've met adult siblings specifically going into disability studies, working for non-profits that help children in the community, become social workers, or even go into healthcare related fields such as occupational therapists and speech therapists. Shocker, right? Their lives are filled with love – they hardly ever put themselves first. Mom, dad... I think it's time we helped them do that.

One other interesting thing that has come up is what the siblings say when we ask them to write down what their fear or worry is at that exact moment. We ask them to write it down before they share it, and then we allow whoever wanted to share tell us why they fear whatever they wrote.

Breaking Through Special Needs

The number one thing they express is the fear of being alone. They express that they are fearful of not being with their family or their sibling, and that when they think about it, it just scares them. In addition, many of them also tell of how scary it is for them to not really know how they will care for their sibling when they get older. I think this says so much about how special these kids truly are.

Remember, these are children themselves: they worry and are fearful of how they will care for their families. They are thinking, feeling, and processing emotions and scenarios that adults typically can't even comprehend. They are at an entirely different maturity level than their peers, which is exactly why they feel they can't relate to them. What other twelve year old is worrying about what their sibling's life will look like in twenty years' time? If you find them, let me know because I don't know any of them. For this reason, you run the risk of viewing your non-special needs children as older than they are: please remember that they're still kids and they desperately need you to support them.

Sadness

Communication is something that I believe most of us take for granted. Our ability to express our emotions, our frustrations, our concerns, our joys, and of course, our needs, is an essential piece of our days. The overwhelming majority of special needs children lack the ability to communicate effectively, *even if they are verbal*.

When we ask siblings about their emotions, sadness often comes up, particularity as it relates to communication. This sadness stems from the fact that they understand that their brother/sister 'acts out' or behaves poorly because of his/her inability to communicate what they really need, want, or how they are feeling. Siblings also express sadness if their brother/sister is completely non-verbal, as they are unable to communicate their basic needs. Are they hungry? Are they tired? Do they not feel well? Siblings very often feel deeply for their brother and sister in this regard. These are all aspects of communication that siblings in our workshops have discussed, and no matter what, they always express how sad it makes them feel. They frequently explained that they wish their sibling had the ability to communicate just so they could help them better. In fact, they often feel so much of their *own* situation would be better if only their brother/sister had the ability to communicate what they need and feel.

Guilt/Shame

We've heard this one too. While siblings feel emotions of embarrassment, anger, and neglect, they'll often also feel guilty for feeling those things. We've even heard them say things such as: "I was so mad because I wanted to go out this weekend, like my parents promised, but I know that they're doing the best they can". We've also heard siblings express that they feel guilty for spending time alone with their parents because they know how much their brother/sister needs their parents. Usually, we hear of the guilt at the end of the sessions, particularly after the siblings have expressed how embarrassed or frustrated they've gotten. They often express that they don't ever want to tell their parents about the guilt. Why? Because they don't want to add more stress to their parents' lives! How selfless.

One of my favorite writers, Brene Brown, writes: "The difference between guilt and shame is guilt is 'I did something bad,' and shame is 'I am a bad person.'" That's an incredibly powerful statement. Siblings often think they shouldn't feel the things they are, and they try to stop themselves really experiencing those emotions. Yet, without being able to express those emotions in a safe space, often keeping them inside and not expressing them, they become more isolated. Hence, these siblings genuinely need the support of peers who understand and are in a similar situation.

Misunderstood

As mentioned earlier, siblings are often misunderstood, as friends don't "get it". Parents may also not be seeing the full scope of their child's emotions because they are entrenched with so many other things going on. In our workshops, siblings frequently explain how their parents often dismiss their anger or frustration, and they feel it's because mom and dad don't understand them; they feel like they haven't done anything wrong.

For me personally, the best example of a situation where this wasn't the case is one I heard from one of our siblings during a workshop we hosted. We were facilitating a discussion based on the times when they

Breaking Through Special Needs

felt embarrassed and asked them to describe the situation and why they felt that way. One of our siblings mentioned how he was going out to dinner with his family and he wanted to be excited, but he knew that his younger sibling would be poorly behaved and likely scream the entire time "like usual". He told us they were in the parking lot outside of the restaurant – as he described the next part, he rolled his eyes – and, with a told-you-so tone, mentioned how his sibling already started yelling. He told us how he refused to go inside because he knew it would be so embarrassing if his sibling yelled indoors.

Now, here at *Breakthrough*, we've heard this of this type of situation multiple times, though the outcomes can sometimes differ. In this particular situation, he mentioned how his dad just said "okay". He told us he was surprised at his father – why didn't he get yelled at? I remembering he smiled at this, though: he was so glad – he felt like his parents just understood him in that moment.

Now, I'm certain you know this *misunderstood* feeling as a parent too. It's interesting how your child's experience as a sibling can almost parallel yours. There are many times the parents of our clients with special needs mention how so many people just don't 'get it', and now, comparing it to the sibling's experience, we see that they, too, think the same of their parents. For you, many day-to-day situations are very different to those of a family without a child with special needs. In this moment, for this one boy, he felt understood. He felt a connection that he'd be longing for from his parents. This was clearly a moment that stands out for him, because he mentioned it even though it wasn't a recent event. He remembers being heard and being understood: this is something we take for granted often, yet it is something rare for members of a family with a special needs child.

Not being part of a "normal family".

Sometimes, being the sibling of a special needs child means sacrificing time with friends or not being able to go out when you, as their parents, can't drive them, for example. It therefore means cancelled birthday parties or trips and going to the ER instead; it means going to doctor visits with their special needs brother/sister instead of getting to play on the playground. Is it any wonder they feel slightly sad at not being part of a 'normal family'?

You, as a parent, can see this for what it is and can offer support – it can make all the difference.

What They Gain

Sure, there are challenges, but remember that there is always a silver lining – I'm sure you know that already. Here's are some of the incredible attributes these very special siblings tend to share:

Empathy

This has to be number one. Sibling of special needs children often experience such hard times with their own family that, when someone else goes through something tough, they *feel* it for them. When our *SibShops* kids share their experiences of something tough or sad, the others listen intently and share in their own feelings with those speaking. It's very special.

Once, not long ago, we asked a question to illicit a discussion based on frustration. One of our siblings recounted his story: all he wanted was to play one particular video game that he hadn't yet played, but his brother kept bothering him. Eventually, his frustration set in and he got into a fight with his brother. He told us that his mom then got angry with him because "his brother doesn't know any better"; she punished him for his outburst. He told us how frustrated this made him and that he doesn't understand why he would be the one getting in trouble when it was his brother that caused it. In his own words, he explained the following: "I'm tired of always being expected to be perfect or blamed for everything".

Wow. Powerful right?

Does any of that sound familiar to you? Maybe you realize that you, too, demonstrate more empathy and concern for your child with special needs than you do for your other children? I'm certainly not judging you, merely pointing you to an area you may not have looked into. Maybe it doesn't, though. All I do know is that we here at *Breakthrough* hear these stories all of the time, and we know that everyone is just trying their best. The point of this is: when this young boy shared his story, the other kids immediately offered support and comforting phrases like "I HATE when

Breaking Through Special Needs

that happens, too". Subsequently, they offered help by relaying what works for them when they experience a situation like that. Even the siblings that weren't able to directly relate to that story were able to listen intently and feel the frustration with the narrating boy.

I have one more story relating to empathy. *Siblings feel empathy for you as their parents, too.* Despite not being able to walk in your shoes, so many of the stories and feelings they relay to us during our workshops relate right back to what you, as a parent, is feeling. It's extremely touching.

During one of our workshops, for example, we played a game with a chart of feelings. The siblings had to roll a ball to a chart on the floor, and whichever feeling it landed on guided them as to a story they'd be encouraged to share. When it was one young girl's turn, she rolled the ball and it landed on 'sadness'. She paused, curled her legs up into her chest, and rested her chin on her knees as she started to share. She asked if it was okay that she didn't describe just one example, but rather spoke of sadness in general. After getting the okay, she started to open up and describe her sadness.

She felt sad that she didn't get that much one-on-one time with her parents. She felt sad that her sister wasn't able to control herself and would often hit her parents when they were trying to help her. She felt sad because she saw how frustrated her mom was when her sister was having a bad day, yet she still tried to smile. She described each of these moments to the group and everyone sat in complete stillness and silence to listen. I will never forget how she told her story, and at the very end of all of that she said, "I feel sad for my parents because I know they are doing their best. I know they have so much to do and it must be so hard for them." How powerful is that? It's likely she's never even opened up to her parents in this way before, either, yet your experiences are paralleled.

Even though she recognized that she goes through hard or frustrating situations, she felt sad for her parents. She felt the sadness that you as her parents feel. Why? Because she sees it every day.

This is not an isolated story... over the years we've heard so many stories just like it. When these children are able to understand someone else's point of view at such a young age, then it is a remarkable propensity to empathize.

They see your struggles and understand. They feel it with you and know you are still doing your best.

Resilience

Siblings are faced with such an added burden, and they encounter situations that a typical child their age never has to… but, they always pull through it. They pull through all of the obstacles placed in front of them and always gain insight and learn from their experiences.

One of our siblings shared his story of strain at home during the pandemic. He knew his parents were overwhelmed at trying to juggle fifty balls in the air at once. As with every household, the COVID-19 situation places so much added strain and stress on them. They are now home with their special needs brother/sister more: as parents, they are trying to play teachers, therapists, mom or dad, and work from home full time. It seems an impossible task.

He shared the stresses going on at home, but then beautifully transitioned into why he knows his family will get through it. He stated,

> We've had to go through so much, with [my sister] being in the hospital for a really long time once and having to manage things then… I know we will be fine through this. I think just during this pandemic people are scared because they don't know if they'll get sick or if it will be bad or not, but we kind of deal with that every day and are okay. I mean it's stressful, but this will pass.

This young boy didn't just come out of the womb with that level of resilience. What a shining light he is.

They've seen you struggle, go through stress, be scared, and face obstacles nearly every single day of their lives… and they've seen you pull through with resilience. They've been able to learn from their hardships because they've seen their parents do it.

Breaking Through Special Needs

They learned it from seeing you, their parents, be resilient.

Responsibility

I do realize that 'responsibility' can also be seen in a negative light. Why? Because siblings gain so much responsibility at such a young age. But, here's the thing: they become so much more independent because of it. They are self-sufficient in many ways and are able to handle things many other kids their age depend on their parents for. I've had parents tell me that it feels like they've cheated their other child out of a "normal" childhood, and maybe their childhood IS different, but they gain so much independence and such a self-sufficient attitude that it will set them up for success in the future. Try to remember that.

Perspective

Facing the hardships that siblings of a special needs child do – at such a young age – is not easy or fair. And that's precisely why I admire how steadfast they are in voicing and adhering to what they value. Many adults have not yet come around to seeing the world in the same incredible light these siblings do. So many adults go day-to-day without valuing the things that really matter in life. In contrast, these siblings value time with their family, time alone, friends that really matter, their health and their family's health, and the little things that mean a whole lot. *They have the same struggles that all other kids their age do, but they see them very differently.* A friend that doesn't accept their sibling for who they are, well, they don't have time for him/her; getting to spend an hour alone with mom or dad... that they cherish; smiles and laughs from their siblings... these are little miracles to them.

Remember, it's not that they don't go through what "typical" children their age go through. It's that they go through that AND then some more, and they truly gain perspective in what matters. They might be disappointed that their birthday party was cancelled because their sibling was sick or had a medical emergency, but it doesn't last: they know that as long as everyone ends up okay and healthy, that's what matters. We could all learn a thing or two from them.

Gratitude

Breaking Through Special Needs

While it's easy for them to sit there and be angry, frustrated, or annoyed at their situations, I often find that when we practice gratitude as a group during our *SibShop* program, the siblings always have gratitude for the simplest and purest of things. Sure, sometimes it's about the video games or a birthday present they got, but often it's the bigger and greater things in life: health, time with family, and time with their brother/sister.

During one of our workshops, we asked them to share their favorite memories. They had to think of a memory that made them really happy. You can probably guess where I'm going with this, right? Yup, nearly all of them referenced a memory that involved their special needs sibling.

One of our young girls told us about a day when her twin brother was laughing uncontrollably. She described how he likes to quote movies and shows and how sometimes she gets annoyed by it, but that day he just happened to quote something really funny and he laughed. She giggled as she told the story, too. At the end of it, she said: "I know it just seems like something that's not very special, but I don't know why, it's just my favorite memory. Seeing him smile and be happy makes me happy."

Another one of our siblings shared a story of when he was playing with his non-verbal younger sister while she was in her chair. He described how normally she would just smile which "is really cute", but on this day she started to laugh. As he shared, he smiled and explained how it was a belly laugh and he never really got to hear her laugh before. He said he's so glad they got it on video – now he can watch it over and over because it just makes him so happy.

Please keep in mind that we said your happiest memory in general. Isn't that incredible? There was no preface to our question and most of the siblings chose stories relating to their brother/sister anyway. We can all see that siblings of special needs children appreciate and are incredibly grateful for all the things that truly matter in life: time, smiles, laughter, and connections.

Lastly, I'd like to share one more moment that always stands out for me. During one of our discussions, we asked the siblings the following: "If you could change your sibling to not have special needs, or change the world in which everyone sees it, which would you choose?"

Breaking Through Special Needs

And guess what? They ALL chose the way the world sees it. They explained that they love their special needs siblings the way they are and wish that people would understand them better. They wish that people didn't stare at them the way they do when they're out in public. They even wish that people could see that, even if they don't talk, or walk, or they act a little 'different', that those are the things that make them special and unique. They wish that people could see how amazing they are even though they are different.

It was such a powerful discussion, and their responses just go to show how special these siblings really are: they see the world in such a different light and are so much better off because of it.

They are just like you.

Mom and dad – your neuro-typical children are allowed to grieve, too. Whether they were born into the situation and are younger, or had their lives changed when the special needs sibling became part of the family, they realize their lives are different. They're allowed to grieve, too. They are allowed to grieve the loss of "normalcy" they see around them. They are allowed to feel just the way they do and it's incredibly important that they realize they are not the only ones feeling that way. Reaching out to a sibling support program is critical in helping them realize this; such a program will provide the support they need. Finding and connecting with other children who also have siblings with special needs allows a non-judgmental sounding board for their worries and frustrations.

According to a 2005 University of Washington Survey of adults who have attended *Sibshops* as kids:

- Over 90% of the respondents said *Sibshops* had a positive effect on the feelings they had for their siblings;
- *Sibshops* taught coping strategies to over two-thirds of respondents;
- 75% reported that *Sibshops* affected their *adult* lives positively;
- 94% said they would recommend *Sibshops* to others.

Those are some pretty strong statistics pointing to the value these children and young adults find in a program like this. Not only did they

Breaking Through Special Needs

benefit during the time of the workshops, but their effects are long-lasting.

I've spoken with so many adult siblings since I've started this program, and they all say they WISH they had a program like SibShops when they were younger. They even wish they had one now... because the journey never really ends. You get older, but the worries, fears, and frustrations just morph into something else. It's the same reason YOU as their parent feel you need support, too.

If we all acted with just a touch of the understanding and patience these siblings demonstrate on a daily basis, the world would be a very different – and arguably better – place. These children's ability to be vulnerable amazes me. The way they open up in the safe space they've been allowed to do so in with others who "get it"… is priceless. Their ability to share emotions, make connections with one another, and speak with poise and understanding – even if they feel they've been mistreated – is remarkable.

They need support, too. Before we move into the next section of this chapter – some powerful stories – I want you to take a moment and reflect on this: siblings of special needs children need support, recognition, and above all, your time and attention, too. It's amazing what special children you have – they would do anything for you and your special needs child. What a wonderful thought to hold close to your heart.

SIBLING STORIES: STORIES FROM THEIR POINT OF VIEW.

I asked some of our *SibShop* kids to share their stories with you as a parent. I wanted them to have the opportunity to share, but also to give you the opportunity to hear it from them. Their stories deserve to be heard, and I hope it will help give clarity and meaning in terms of your family life.

Owen

My name is Owen. I'm from Wading River, New York, and I'm 13 years old. I love cars and playing video games. My brother's name is Elliot. He has a rare chromosome disorder. He is not able to communicate with anyone. He also can't hear without hearing aids. He also has an intellectual disability that makes learning and development more difficult than normal.

Breaking Through Special Needs

Having a sibling with special needs can be challenging at times, no doubt about it. Because of my brother's special needs, my parents have little to no free time throughout the day to relax or spend time with me. As a result of that, I have a lot more responsibilities than other kids my age.

However, being extra responsible isn't exactly a BAD thing. Because of my brother, I'm more set up for the future. I'm able to do more things on my own than other kids. I'm also more selfless and understanding of others. Whenever I'm out in public and I see somebody with special needs, I'll always smile and wave hello because I understand what they might have to go through every day. The world is so harsh on people that are "different", and they don't deserve that.

I think that other kids who have siblings with special needs need to know one thing: life has its ups, and downs, but one thing that will never change is the relationship you have with your sibling. They may not be able to tell you, or show you, but your sibling will always love you. They look up to you. They care about you. And sometimes, life may not seem so fair. But, remember: everything always works out in the end.

Peyton

Hi! My name is Peyton Waszkiewicz. I am from Long Island, and I am 14 years old. I have been doing karate for 7 years and I am a half black belt. I have also been doing horseback riding for 3 years. In my free time, I enjoy drawing and watching Anime. I am not much of a fan of running. My family consists of my mom and dad, my 11 year old sister, Emerson, and my 5 year old sister Kylie. My sister Emerson was diagnosed with autism, epilepsy, and CDD, which is a very rare neurological disorder.

Being a sibling of a sister with special needs has taught me to be more patient and accepting of others. I am much more mature and independent. The hardest part about being a sib with a sister with special needs is not being able to understand my sister's wants and needs. Not understanding her creates more problems because she gets upset and throws tantrums. I feel that not being able to know what she wants makes me feel like a bad sister for not knowing how to make her happy, but I know at the moment this cannot be helped.

Breaking Through Special Needs

In these 11 years, I have made tons of memories with my sister. There are scary times and happy times. Once when my grandmother was visiting from Florida, my parents went out to eat and left us home. We heard Emmy scream, so we checked the cameras and it looked like she was having a seizure, so we went into her room. I feel scared and helpless when she is having a seizure because there is not much that we can do but watch and wait for the seizure to end. Emerson has a gray horse and she always has it with her. So sometimes, in stores, she will walk up to strangers and try to give them her horse, and sometimes she will be loud in stores and we will get lots of stares, and stuff like that can be embarrassing. And times where me, Emmy, and my other younger sister are all cooperating, we can have a lot of fun playing together. Getting to see my sisters smile while all of us are playing together is amazing!

I have told most of my friends about Emmy and her disabilities, so they are aware of what it will be like if I invite them over. Most of my friends are accepting of her, which is good. If my friends do come over, Emmy will usually show interest in them and try to play with them with her horse and then we would go hang out somewhere else.

I feel like my relationship with Emerson is different than someone with a typical sibling. For example, I cannot have a normal conversation and she cannot voice her opinion or what she wants. She has a lot of people helping her such as aides, nurses, therapists, and teachers in our home over the years, which differs from my friends with typical siblings.

I want my parents to know that I am always here to help if they need it and that I love them so much!

The biggest lesson I have learned from being a sib with special needs is just to try to be the best person you can be, and be kind and accepting to everyone.

Ryan

My name is Ryan DeSimone. I live in Nesconset, New York, and I am thirteen years old. My likes include playing hockey with my friends and playing the piano for my friends and family. I also enjoy playing video games and bike riding. One of my biggest dislikes is injustice and things that are deemed unfair. Although I may seem like an ordinary kid with an ordinary life, that is not the case. My special needs sister, Katelynn, has made my life truly special and as far from "ordinary" as possible.

Breaking Through Special Needs

My family is made up of my mother, father, sister, and me. We have always loved each other and have grown stronger during the hardest of times. Nevertheless, we have constantly found difficulty in balancing our time with school, working, extracurricular activities, and taking care of my ten year old sister, Katelynn. Katelynn has a rare form of epilepsy known as CDKL5 Deficiency Disorder. Also known as CDD, it limits her in many ways such as preventing her from speaking and performing simple tasks that we all take for granted. She cannot speak or use her hands to support or help herself. In addition, she is unable to feed herself and must be spoon-fed purees. She is also unable to walk or even sit up on her own. Everything must be done for Katelynn, and she requires nurses throughout the morning and until the evening for daily care. CDKL5 also causes her to have multiple seizures throughout the day, which can last anywhere from one second to five minutes. As a result, she takes a variety of medications which do not always work effectively and cause her to feel weak and tired. She has little energy and can barely muster up the strength to roll over.

Despite this, Katelynn has overcome many trials of adversity and continues to inspire her family and others. Having such a strong and determined little sister has given me strengths that I would not have had otherwise. For example, she taught me to be understanding and conscious of other people's situations. In other words, I try my best to not judge a book by its cover and I give people the benefit of the doubt. While some people may give off a critical opinion with a glance to those who do not look similar to them, I try not to judge and I give them a friendly smile. Having a special needs sister has also made me more resilient. Katelynn has gone through many struggles throughout her life and has been challenged by her disorder in a multitude of ways. She must constantly put up with violent seizures and daily therapies in order to regain the strength she lost during her previous seizure. She always seems to be playing catch-up with small milestones when dealing with constant seizures. Despite this, she has defied the odds and prevailed in every challenge that she has had to face. As Katelynn faces these challenges, it forces me to remain strong and hopeful. Although her hardships may be stressful, they force me to become a stronger person. Her resilience inspires me to be stronger.

Finally, being a brother to my special needs sister has taught me to be more grateful and thankful for what I have. My sister's condition forces my family to devote much of our time to tending to her. Although many people may feel sympathetic towards us, I always remember that many people are in an even worse situation than we are in. There are families who have lost family members with special needs, and Katelynn is still with us. Even though our circumstances may not be the greatest, I give thanks that Katelynn is still with her family.

Breaking Through Special Needs

Having a sister with special needs has taught me the valuable life lesson of not judging a book by its cover and has made me a more understanding and strong-willed person. However, being a brother to Katelynn can prove to be extremely difficult at times. The hardest part of having a special needs sister is watching her struggle during her lowest points. Katelynn has faced several lows throughout her life, such as when she fell ill to pneumonia several times, or when she went into status epilepticus. Nevertheless, she has achieved many accomplishments throughout her life considering her severe condition. Some of her achievements include sipping from a straw for the first time and using her communication device, the Tobii. Alongside her triumphs, she has also had to endure countless seizures throughout her life - and multiple hospitalizations. Whenever Katelynn experiences more seizures than usual, she is forced to work harder to accomplish the same task. This can be very stressful to those around her, her family.

It is hard for me to endure when she is being hospitalized. It is hard for me to accept that she has so many seizures and that I cannot do anything to help her besides being there for her and holding her hand. To make matters worse, her disorder also makes her immune system less effective and more susceptible to illnesses and viruses. Coughs, fevers, bronchitis, and pneumonia have all been great threats to my sister over the course of her life. It ticks me off to know that most people can easily withstand these illnesses while my sister must fight for her life after catching one. She is at an extreme disadvantage and is threatened by the smallest of sicknesses. Nevertheless, she always perseveres and beats any challenge or sickness that she encounters.

Being a sibling of somebody so tough and special has left me with quite a few stories over the past ten years. One of my most memorable experiences with Katelynn took place when I was only five years old. Katelynn went into status epilepticus, which is a continuous seizure lasting more than 30 minutes, or two or more seizures without regaining consciousness between any of them. She was immediately rushed to the Neonatal Intensive Care Unit (NICU) and treated while I stayed at my grandparents' house. We had hoped she would be released quickly, but our hopes were slowly crushed as the days passed by. Although the prolonged hospitalization became difficult for me to handle, the stress that it put on my parents was devastating. In order to keep constant supervision on my sister and me, my parents took turns taking off from work and taking care of us. As time progressed, it became increasingly difficult for them to keep switching between us and work, and they hoped that Katelynn would soon recover and be released from the hospital.

Finally, Katelynn was taken home one month after she was first brought to the hospital. It relieved the large amount of stress that was put on my parents and allowed our lives to go back to normal. Unfortunately, this experience had lasting effects on Katelynn and would set her back in many ways. For example, she could no longer sit

Breaking Through Special Needs

up alone or sip from a straw. These are milestone skills that she has yet to regain seven years later. Although Katelynn has had many negative experiences in the past, she has also had lots of fun and positive experiences as well. Although my sister is unable to do much, she sometimes surprises us with things we never knew she was capable of doing. For instance, Katelynn once laughed for two straight minutes! About one year ago, my sister was sitting in her chair with my grandmother and me in the kitchen. Out of nowhere, we heard what seemed to be giggling from the other side of the room. When we looked to see what it was, we were shocked to see my sister gleefully laughing! It was amazing to see my sister being so happy. She had never laughed for more than 15 seconds before, and I had never been there to see it. I was amazed that her laugh sounded like that of a typical girl's. It was impossible to spot any differences between Katelynn's laugh and a typical nine-year old girl's laugh. The memory still continues to amaze me to this day.

Having a special needs sister has proven to be difficult to handle over the course of my life, especially while watching her struggle through her lowest points. Nonetheless, I have had many memorable experiences with Katelynn and have gathered many different stories. Having a special needs sister can change people's perspectives on you and your family. Since Katelynn is unable to do many things, such as walking and talking, many of my friends do not know her. She goes unnoticed whenever my friends come to my house to play or talk. I have many friends with special needs siblings whose relationships were changed dramatically by their siblings. Unlike them, I feel like my relationships with my friends without special needs siblings are unaffected by my sister. However, I always become frustrated when friends of mine complain about their siblings. Almost all of my friends tend to gripe and complain about how their siblings can be so annoying and irritating at times. They often get angry after their siblings make the tiniest of mistakes and wish they wouldn't bother them at all. For example, something as meaningless as one sibling changing the channel on the TV while the other sibling is watching it, or teasing, can provoke arguments with each other. However, they do not realize how truly lucky they are to even have the ability to converse or play with their siblings! None of my friends who have siblings without special needs ever show any gratitude for being able to even talk to their siblings whatsoever! They have never considered what their lives would be like while having siblings with special needs.

I find it irritating how much my friends take for granted when complaining about their siblings. There are people across the world who are unable to properly communicate with their siblings because of disorders limiting their abilities, yet they still gripe about meaningless things. I would like to let my friends know that they should be grateful for being able to communicate and play with their siblings. Unfortunately, not everybody is *given the ability to speak or play with their siblings. Even if siblings can be somewhat annoying at times, you should always show gratitude for having a sibling you can communicate with. Words can bring people together, but also push them apart. Although my sister does not typically affect my relationships with my friends without siblings with special needs, it is undeniable that my relationship with my sister differs greatly from a typical sibling relationship. For example, my sister and I never grow apart from each other or fight with each other, while others always find themselves arguing with their siblings for various different reasons.*

Since Katelynn and I are unable to properly communicate with each other, we often pass the time by just being next to each other and keeping each other company. We always stay calm while together and have never been sour towards each other in our entire lives. When she has a seizure, I am always by her side until it is over. Many times, I cuddle up next to her and watch her favorite shows on TV. We are always peaceful towards each other and love relaxing together. Contrarily, typical siblings constantly tease, hold grudges against each other, and argue about meaningless things. As previously stated, they constantly complain about one another and tease each other. Although many other siblings have healthy and strong relationships and do not always fight, they still differ from the relationship with my sister. The lack of being able to communicate results in a relaxed, calm relationship that differs from many other typical sibling relationships.

In addition, my relationship with Katelynn differs from a typical sibling relationship because of our inability to share our thoughts with each other and solve issues together. Despite the fact that our lack of communication results in a relaxed relationship, it can be frustrating to not know what could be bothering Katelynn in a situation where she needs help. For example, if she is hungry or has pain somewhere in her body, she cannot tell me what is troubling her. I cannot solve the issue if she is unable to tell me what the problem is in the first place. I often have to guess what she needs, which typically does not resolve the issues. On the other hand, siblings are able to solve their problems by communicating with each other and rationalizing solutions. Although siblings undoubtedly argue frequently, they are still able to work together in order to solve issues. They could tell each other if they had pain or were hungry. Unlike my sister and I, typical siblings are able to share their thoughts and feelings with each other. Even if it may be difficult not being able to understand my sister at times, we carry on and have a unique and peaceful relationship that typical siblings do not have with each other.

Having a sister with special needs has drastically changed my life for the better. She has helped me become a more understanding and resilient person and taught me valuable life lessons. The nonverbal relationship we have with each other does not

Breaking Through Special Needs

interfere with any of my own relationships with friends and is very unique when compared to a typical sibling relationship. Albeit her lack of communication can be frustrating to deal with, we still make it work. However, since Katelynn is unable to do many things by herself, my parents must sacrifice their time to help and support her. They are challenged to balance their time with Katelynn and me. I am sometimes shocked at how well they are able to balance their long hours with time spent taking care of Katelynn and being with me! I am lucky to have such amazing parents. They also do a great job with spending time with me in addition to tending to Katelynn. This is a problem that many parents of special needs children have trouble confronting and dealing with.

I would like to let my parents know that they are doing a fantastic job juggling their time spent at their jobs and time spent with Katelynn and me! They must tend to Katelynn's everyday needs, such as feeding, changing, therapies, and keeping on top of medical visits. Also, they must consistently prepare and feed meals to Katelynn and give her the proper amount of each medication she takes every day. They take Katelynn to multiple different specialists, such as an orthopedist, pediatrician, neurologist, orthotist, endocrinologist, intensive therapy, music therapy, and more! It can be extremely stressful to deal with at times, yet they continue to do it without missing a beat. They are always there for us, and I think Katelynn would agree with me if I said that we couldn't have better parents!

Finally, I would like other siblings like me to know that no matter how negative your situation may be, or no matter how hopeless you may feel, you must be resilient and stay strong. If your special needs sibling is faced with a daunting challenge or a tough situation, you must remain strong with him. When Katelynn experiences a high number of seizures in a short amount of time, I choose to stay by her side and be strong with her. Having a special needs sister has taught me a multitude of valuable lessons: the most valuable lesson was to always stay strong. Remember that there are thousands of other people who have siblings with special needs who all experience similar issues and dilemmas. Being a big brother to a sister with special needs can prove to be difficult at times. It can be extremely stressful and frustrating. Nevertheless, Katelynn continues to enrich my family's lives with valuable life lessons and strengths. She brings joy to our hearts with a simple smile. Katelynn has taught many meaningful lessons and has truly transformed my life for the better.

Adelaide

What is your name, where are you from, how old are you?

Adelaide Knight, Rochester NY, 5

Breaking Through Special Needs

Tell us about your likes and dislikes, what you like to do for fun!

Likes: toys, play outside, pink, Sofia the First
Dislikes: squash, washing my hair, chores

Tell us about your family, how old is your sibling with special needs, what is their diagnosis?

Preston is 13 and has Autism, Mommy, Daddy, and Mathias is 2.

What do you think your strengths are from having a sibling with special needs?

More independent.

What do you think is the hardest part about having a sibling with special needs?

Sometimes he's not nice.

Tell us some stories about being a sibling – scary times, fun times, embarrassing times, whatever you'd like!

This summer, I was playing outside with Preston in the sprinkler. We took turns using my Paw Patrol water squirter.

What are some things you would want your parents to know?

Sometimes he's mean to me. When Preston has a meltdown I feel upset.

Biggest lesson, what do you want other siblings like you to know?

When you need help, ask your parents!

Breaking Through Special Needs

Maintaining a Healthy Lifestyle

It's time to find out how you can do the very best for your child by maintaining healthy lifestyles across the board. We've heard so many parents struggling with the various parts of this and feeling lost, so I want to provide more resources to help you in any way possible! Ready? Let's jump in.

Have you ever heard that the *Department of Health* recommends that we, as adults, get at least 150 minutes of moderate aerobic activity each week? You've probably heard about the negative long term effects of prolonged sitting, too, right? My guess is that you have, but probably haven't paid it too much attention – after all, you're incredibly busy. The thing is, it is really, really important to make physical activity a priority. And here's the real scare… I have always asked myself the following: "If WE are supposed to be getting that much physical activity and prevent long term sitting, WHY are children and adults with neurological impairments only getting thirty minutes two times a week at school or in their home!?" It gets me every time.

We'll get back to that, but before we do, let's take a little detour. If you are reading this as a parent, then you likely already know the term **neuroplasticity**. In case you don't, though, neuroplasticity is defined as "the brain's ability to reorganize itself by forming new neural connections throughout life" (Bergland, 2017). What this means is that, although our brains have the connections they do now, we are able to change and shape our brains into learning new ideas, ways of doing things, ways to move our bodies, etc. This happens inside all of us, and even our children – or adults with any kind of damage to their brains – can change their neurological pathways in this respect. Your brain can make new connections around the damaged areas, or different parts of your brain can function in ways it normally wouldn't have done simply by "picking up" some of skills that may have been lost or undeveloped.

This is exactly how we learn new skills. For example, we may go to the gym and try to learn a new exercise. It may take several times to do it correctly spontaneously, but once you're able to do it, your brain has formed new connections. This is all because of the brain's plasticity. In terms of re-wiring the brain, then, it works the same way, and this approach is incredibly useful for cognitive growth and learning new ideas.

It's no different when it comes to our neuro-impaired children. Because their brains are wired a little differently, or have damaged areas, it just takes a little longer. It takes more repetitions and consistent retraining to be able to learn a new task – both cognitive and physical ones – but, it can definitely be done. *Slower learning is still learning.*

Having said that, let's get back to the first part of this chapter: why, then, are children and adults with neurological impairments only granted 30 minutes a few times a week for their therapies or activities? Why, when pathways can be altered and behaviors can be modified, do they not get given more time to improve their lifestyles?

The answer is a sad one, and I have to admit that I get incredibly angry over it: insurance and governmental policies won't pay for more time. It's an unfortunate truth that the political powers believe they know more than the actual clinicians and specialists your children work with on a daily basis. Have you sensed the frustration in my writing yet? It's KNOWN that these kids need more, but it's not talked about. It's not mentioned that schools only give two sessions a week to a child with serious physical and cognitive delay. And it's not talked about because "nobody gets that much approved"; if you do, it's because you've had to advocate so strongly – and potentially even threaten a law suit – for YOUR OWN CHILD'S RIGHTS. Sometimes I really question whether this is real life. Why do you need to go to such great lengths just to get even a quarter of what your child deserves? Why do you need to celebrate the fact that you got four sessions approved in a week instead of two?

It should never be a fight. And if I sound angry, it's because I am.

I don't, however, want to focus on the negatives. Your child, even if he/she is not overtly physically compromised, still needs regular physical activity for his/her overall health. So many parents tell me how their children live sedentary lifestyles, how their kids want to play video games, sit on their *iPads*, or just aren't motivated to do any sort of physical activity. In addition, there are families that have children who struggle

Breaking Through Special Needs

with physical disabilities and their mobility. It is all the same, though... they ALL need exercise, just like we do!

Improving Behaviors, Motivation, and Overall Health

We already know that exercise promotes a healthy weight, strong bones, reduces stress, and improves overall cardiovascular function. What you might not already know, however, is that it provides benefits for behaviors, too! In addition to better blood circulation throughout your body, during exercise your brain actually releases neurotransmitters. Okay, I promise not to get too "science-y", but these neurotransmitters actually help our brains function. To connect the dots, exercise actually helps your brain work better! And if it's good for you, then guess what? It's good for your special needs child, too!

ADHD and ASD

It's a huge blessing that exercise is effective for neuro-impaired children and adults, both. Several studies have, in fact, looked at the effects of exercise on individuals with ADHD and have proven that it improves attention, concentration, and organizational skills! And that's not running a marathon... it's by doing small bouts of exercise regularly. One other study tested forty children with ADHD by placing them into an *exercise* group and a *control* group. Participants in the *exercise* group performed moderately intense aerobic exercise for 30 minutes, while the control group watched a running or exercise related video. With specific assessments, they were able to measure that the children with ADHD in the *exercise* group **improved on their assessments** when measuring attention and non-perseverative scores; this was directly compared to the control group which demonstrated no significant changes in their scores (Healy, 2018)

Yet another study measured the effects of exercise for ADHD and ASD by studying children with these disorders as well as without. After just 20 minutes of exercise, all the kids – children with ADHD, ASD, or no diagnoses – improved their behavior, thinking skills, and school performance. In fact, the children with ADHD and ASD showed additional improved self-control and decreased impulsive behaviors.

Overall, these studies illustrate that exercise reduces problem behaviors such as repetitive behaviors, off-task behavior, mouthing, self-injury, disruptiveness, and aggression. The benefits can also produce a positive feedback loop. What does that mean? Well, it means that, over time, the more they do exercise, the better their bodies respond to it and will continue to benefit from it!

The *Journal of Behavioral Nutrition and Physical Activity* conducted a systematic review of the health benefits related to physical activity and fitness in school, specifically with regard to young children and youths. In this review, they found that physical activity was associated with numerous health benefits including, though not limited to, improved bone health, improved cardiovascular function, and improved mood. This study in particular indicates that the more physical activity children do, the greater the health benefits available to them.

When it comes to children with ASD, specifically, a meta-analysis concludes that physical interventions have a positive effect on a variety of outcomes, including the following: development of manipulative skills, locomotor skills, skill-related fitness, social functioning, and muscular strength and endurance. This allows us to come to the conclusion that physical activity and exercise can serve as an evidence-based strategy for youth with ASD.

So, what does a review of all of these studies mean, and more importantly, what does it mean for your child? Well, all of these studies underscore that exercise has positive effects for everybody, though it can improve overall function and regulation of children with ASD and ADHD, specifically. You, as parents of a child with ASD or a related neurological diagnosis, struggle with behaviors constantly. I understand this. So, I challenge you to do the following: instead of increasing or switching medications, why not try a natural approach to improving the function and abilities of your special needs child? This is in no way saying that medications are bad, or that you should never use them. Not at all. I'm merely suggesting adding another tool to your toolbox so that that you can refer back to it if it ultimately helps your child be the best version of themselves.

Why, though, is the benefit of exercise not talked about more often? I wish I knew the answer to that. Many doctors automatically administer

Breaking Through Special Needs

pain medications, injections, or advise surgery rather than trying any other approaches first, particularly when it comes to chronic pain in adults. Similarly, children are often medicated or given 'treatments' that are simply not natural to the human body. Could it hurt, then, to try an exercise program? Unless there are significant precautions related to your child's health, it most definitely couldn't. If you're unsure, though, it's always best to speak with a specialist before beginning any program.

IMPROVING SOCIAL SKILLS

On a daily basis, I speak with parents who are concerned about their childrens'' social interactions and social skills. So many of them seek out social skill classes, yet find little to no benefit in them. They often tell me how frustrating it is that they are unable to improve in this area. So, would you believe me if I told you that fitness also improves social skills and communication? It's true!

The same meta-analysis cited above concludes that structured physical fitness programs showed significant gains in social and communication skills. The environment, in particular, must be a safe one and fun setting in which children and adults can learn. Group physical activity settings offer amazing opportunities to practice social skills. Activities such as these are opportunities to interact nonverbally as well as verbally... all while having fun! Social skills groups are amazing programs for kids with special needs, but more so, in combination with programs that encourage physical activities. (Healy, 2018)

IMPROVING OVERALL FITNESS AND MOTOR SKILLS

Due to the repercussions of sedentary lifestyles, difficulty performing physical activities, and negative behaviors, children with ASD are at greater risk for obesity (Zuckerman, 2014). Prevalence of obesity in the pediatric population, we know, is increasing. Evidence suggests that children with ASD and ADHD may be at much greater risk. Out of over 5,000 participants in one study, it was illustrated that amongst the children with ASD, 33.6% were overweight and 18% were obese. Guess what that total equals: over FIFTY PERCENT of children with ASD are overweight or obese (Hill, 2015) This compares to statistics in neuro-typical children ages 2-18 years old where 20.6% are overweight and

18.6% of the population are obese - totaling **36% being overweight and obese – according to the CDC.**

Aren't those numbers scary? Yes. Is there something we can do about it, though? Yes, thankfully. I'm sure you aren't really surprised by those numbers, but remember, if you are a parent of a child with ASD or ADHD, and you suspect your child is overweight or obese, it doesn't mean you should feel guilty. I'm here to help and explain things. So, let's look into why these numbers can be so high amongst these kids.

First, I'm sure you know that you need good sleep patterns to be able to function well. So does your child. But, do you also know that a lack of sleep could be associated with weight gain? (Hill, 2015) Your metabolism doesn't function at its best when your body is tired. I can't tell you how many times I've heard from worried parents that their children have trouble sleeping at night – this most definitely has a negative impact on the child's weight.

Secondly, special needs children generally have less muscle strength and endurance. In my estimation, they also lack muscle tone. According to a study from 2014, during which physical fitness levels were measured in adolescent males both with ASD and Autism, adolescents with ASD had significantly lower scores on all fitness and motor proficiency measures when compared to the adolescents without ASD. This study urged interventions in order to maximize physical fitness and motor proficiency for adolescents with ASD (Pan 2014). It can therefore be gathered that children and adults with Autism tend to have decreased muscle strength and endurance when compared to a neuro-typical individual of the same age (Janssen, 2014).

Third up is motor planning. You may be wondering what in the world this is. Well, motor planning is simply the brain's ability to take information in, process it, and tell the body how to perform it. For example, pretend that you're learning how to do something new... let's say, for example, that you're learning how to chop an onion correctly. You watch a quick *YouTube* video on how to do it and then you're able to carry out the task, right? Yes, but if you have difficulty motor planning, you may watch the *YouTube* video, but your brain still will not quite *connect the dots*.

Breaking Through Special Needs

How can poor motor planning be helped, then? Well, one way is to break the information down into manageable chunks: watch a video broken down into 'baby steps', for example. In other words, you'd watch a small step, then perform it; you'd then watch another one, and perform, and so forth until the entire task is completed. Children and adults with ASD or ADHD often have trouble motor planning. Even with demonstrations, the task seems confusing to them: their brains don't always send the correct signals.

To bring the point home, I'd like to use squats as an example. Many of the children and adults can barely do these correctly despite the general concept being understood. Even after multiple rounds of demonstration, it's a really tough task for them to do. So it's understandable that, when I ask participants in my group fitness classes to perform squats, I'll inevitably get at least one child or adult who doesn't perform it correctly: they might keep their legs straight and bend to touch the ground with their arms, or they may bends their knees slightly, keep their backs upright, and not bend at the waist. Both of these compensations are classic examples of incorrect squatting posture. In fact, they are also perfect examples of difficulty motor planning. We see that, even after demonstration, squatting is a tough concept to grasp for some. So, when someone has difficulty with this movement in class, we help by tapping on a chair and pretending to sit down: this facilitates the correct movement pattern. These broken down visual clues work wonders.

So, given all of this, here's a challenge for you: imagine that you, yourself, are trying to teach your special needs child something new. Really picture it.

He/she is potentially overweight and having trouble sleeping through the night – even melatonin might not work. He/she has weaker endurance and muscle strength than other kids his/her age, so daily activities that feel easy for you and I seem more challenging for him/her... and he/she gets tired more quickly. Now, add in the fact that, if you try to teach the new, different exercises, his/her daily routine is disrupted. You know where I'm heading with this, right? His/her structure is changed, the routine is broken... looks like we've got a recipe for disaster folks!

Please remember that this doesn't mean *ALL* children and adults with special needs diagnoses have similar problems: many are able to perform really high level exercises and activities. I'm merely trying to give an overview of the large majority of special needs children and adults. From my experience in working on fitness programs with children and adults all over the globe, I can absolutely attest to these common themes. That's why they're right here in my book! Strength and endurance are important for physical health, of course, but they are also vital for taking advantage of social opportunities like involvement in recreational sports, games, or even structured classes!

That having been said, how can you help your child overcome these obstacles? I understand that it can seem an insurmountable mountain to climb, but I'm here to help. Take a look at the following guidance:

Where to Start…

Start Small

The CDC recommends that children get at least one hour of physical activity a day. Is it realistic to start there? Maybe… and maybe not. It could be a big goal for you in your current situation, so I suggest that you start with simply finding something your child likes to do and during which he/she won't be distracted. Start small. For example, for us at *Breakthrough*, we have 30 and 60 minute options. Why? Well, because we realize that not every child or adult can start with completing a full hour. Sometimes, too, there's so much activity already built into their schedules that finding a full hour can be tough. Regardless of what you try first, though, just start!

Sample Different Types of Activities

What does your child really enjoy? Is it being around animals? Maybe it's music. It could even be walking in the park. We've encouraged so many of the families we work with to incorporate additional fitness and physical activity into their days – oftentimes simply by exploring what their children love to do. Some have added walking at the park to feed the ducks, or walking to a favorite bench to sit by the water, into their days. Others have found that horseback riding, theater, or even dance classes work! The options SHOULD BE limitless. However, I do realize that having these types of programs accessible to you in your

Breaking Through Special Needs

communities can be tough. There might just not be enough programs out there to really support your community.

So, if you're having trouble finding a program that meets the criteria of inclusivity, encourages fitness, involves social interaction, and helps special needs children become more independent, then just reach out to me at info@breakthroughptli.com. Here at *Breakthrough Intensive PT*, we have fitness programs doing just that, all of which service kids around globe. Just because your community doesn't offer what you're looking for doesn't mean you can't find an alternative method, right here!

If you are currently looking for a program in your community, though, I encourage you to think about the following tips:
Find someone who understands. At the end of the day, you want your child to have an instructor or facilitator who understands how to communicate and motivate children who learn differently. Communication and patience are key when working with the special needs population and not everybody is able to work effectively to help bring out the best in them. Make sure you search for the right fit for your child; don't settle for less because you think he/she is your only option, especially when the programs offered are obviously few and far between.

Make it a routine. Remember, your child might resist the new exercise at first. He/she might not want to be part of a program and they might struggle with adding something new into his/her schedule. Remember, I may even be hard for him/her, so resistance is fairly natural. When was the last time you found exercise super easy? Every single one of us functions better as part of a routine, especially your child. If you build a predictable structure, your child will benefit even more. Don't give up if it's hard for him/her. Fitness will be challenging – it should be and that's the point – but, the more you create a routine, the easier it will become.

Make it visual. When I instruct our group fitness classes, both in person and virtually, demonstration is key. Demonstration is, in fact, critical. Why? Because children with special needs often have a harder time understanding verbal cues – remember the motor planning section? They function best with visual examples. You could, for example, create a *visual schedule* and fit it into their routines. This can also help them overcome a feeling of being overwhelmed by the new entries in their routines.

Breaking Through Special Needs

I realize that adding new things into your child's routine can be tough. So, I'd like to share a quick story with you before we move on:

A general question people ask when they call the clinic is what our fitness programs cost. Reasonable, right? Callers want to know if they can afford a program and if it's worth pursuing. I've spoken with so many parents who ask this question, but do you know what the question really means? It means that the parents aren't really sure of the value this class has quite yet. In other words, they don't know how it could help them or change their family's life. The thing is, though, I understand their hesitation.

In fact, I'm similar in many ways. If I'm honest, every time I've been concerned about cost, I usually don't end up doing it. Whether it's a trip somewhere, or whether I'm buying something new – cost matters. But why? Well, it's because my mind is so focused on what the cost is that I end up losing sight of the value. Let me tell you about the day that everything changed for me...

On that day, I was telling a friend of mine about how my favorite gym had closed down. I was devastated, as the only existing one near my home was around seven times more expensive per month. That's a big difference! I explained that I was frustrated – after all, why couldn't I just get the same rate I was paying? Well, I didn't want to pay that amount of money, so I haphazardly tried to work out from home... I'm not sure if you've tried doing this, but for me – it's a no go.

After telling my friend all about my frustrations, he turned to me and surprised me with his response: "yeah, but what's it costing you NOT to buy a membership at this new gym?" And boom. Everything changed. My mind started thinking about all of the things I value... my health, my fitness, my strength, my energy levels, etc. I suddenly realized that I was missing out on all of those things because I was too busy worrying about the cost. I'd lost sight of the value! When it came down to it, I immediately realized that I needed to make the gym work with my budget. Why? Because what I'd gain is precisely what I value: maintaining my health, fitness, and energy. And *that's* what I really want out of my life.

Yes, cost matters. But, don't forget about the value of quality programs for your child.

Breaking Through Special Needs

BE A ROLE MODEL

Whether your child is verbal, non-verbal, or whatever the case may be… he/she looks at you, his/her parents and caregivers, as role models. If they see you enjoying physical activity, then it encourages him/her to be positive about it, too. Even aides and assistants who may work with your child can play a significant role in his/her motivation for new fitness activities and routines.

ONE MORE POINT: PROLONGED SITTING AND ITS NEGATIVE EFFECTS

In addition to incorporating more fitness into your child's routine, it's important to tackle general sedentary activities, too.

We all know that sitting for prolonged periods of time is not good for our overall health. We also know, especially after reading the above, that exercise is necessary for our overall health and abilities. So, why is it that there aren't ample resources and opportunities for more medically fragile children and adults – or physically impaired individuals – to get out of their chairs and get moving?

Sure, it's likely that these children, in particular, receive PT and get up thanks to the diligent work that you do as a parent. But, if we calculate the total amount of time they are not in their chairs or seated, it doesn't add up to much. In fact, let's test that. Let's calculate figures for a week. Imagine your child does the following per day:

- 30 minutes of PT at school.
- 30 minutes of PT at home.
- 30 minutes of OT where he/she is out of his/her chair.
- 1 hour in a stander.
- 1 hour in a gait trainer.

This is a very optimistic prediction, and that's only 3.5 hours of his/her chair per day. That means, out of the 12 hour day that he/she is awake, only 25% of it is spent out of a chair! The remaining 75% is spent sitting in an adaptive chair, wheelchair, or strollers.

Breaking Through Special Needs

It isn't good for us, as neuro-typical adults, to sit for 75% of our days. Our neuro-impaired children and adults most definitely shouldn't be seated for that long. I know that you feel as though alternative outcomes are limited. I get it. There's only so much time in a day and only so much you can do. So, I'm not highlighting this statistic to make you feel poorly about how much your child may or may not sit. I am, however, pointing out that there is potential for improvement in this department. By facing the harsh reality that your child is seated for so much of their day, it may bring to the forefront of your mind that this sedentary lifestyle has a significant impact on his/her overall health, bone density, strength, and endurance. Small changes make a large difference.

Aside from all of that, special needs kids deserve social interactions, too! I've already highlighted how important social interaction is in a previous chapter, so won't dwell on it here. Please remember, you're not alone. Finding inclusive programs can be challenging – sometimes it's a bit like searching for a thumb tack in New York City... it might be there, but you're going to have a really hard time finding it on the streets – but, it's not impossible.

As a helping hand, and in case you feel at a loss as to where to start, we have those services at *Breakthrough*. I'd be more than happy to point you in the right direction. Simply reach out to me at info@breakthroughptli.com. Our programs are designed to make up for what others lack... support, community, socialization, and, what's more, another opportunity to get your child out of their chairs and moving; they'll even learn techniques that you can do at home, too. This truly will change both your life and theirs.

As we move to the next chapter, I want to reiterate how incredibly important incorporating exercise into your child's routine is. Fitness should be added into his/her schedule EVERY SINGLE DAY. I know that you won't let anything hold you back from helping your child be the best version of themselves – that's why you're reading this – so, I also know you'll make fitness a prerequisite for your child's development moving forward.

Find a program that is a good fit and you'll never regret it.

Incorporating Home Exercises: For PT and General Fitness

Having spoken extensively about how important physical exercise is for your special needs child, it's time to gain a deeper understanding of what that is and how to do it. Now, I know what you are all thinking: "AH-HA... she's proved she's a therapist writing this book after all." ☺ I'm here to help, so keep an open mind and let's get going.

Let's jump straight in and chat about the dreaded home exercise programs you get from your child's school or home therapists. I think it's worth point out that the first issue, here, is that your life is incredibly busy: you literally have so much going on that, despite how much you genuinely *want to do the* programs, you have difficulty finding the time to *actually do them*. Am I right? Well, let's ease into grappling with issue. I'd like to start with some background help and knowledge that will help you better understand the *why* behind some exercises. The better you understand the *why*, the better you'll be able to do activities and fit them in more effortlessly into your schedule.

Always aim to understand the OUTCOME you're seeking. This is very, very important. Imagine that you're practicing pulling to sit, or even a stretching position with your child. Ask yourself the following: "What is this going to help my child do?" Powerful, right?

If you do activities with your child while keeping the outcome in mind, it will make it easier to commit to doing them consistently. And when I say 'outcome', I don't mean "getting their core stronger" or "their muscles looser". While good, what I really mean is keeping in mind how the activity is going to help them overall – what is it going to help them to do? Is it going to help them sit by themselves one day? Is it going to loosen their muscles so they don't scissor their legs when they stand? Is it going to help them prevent scoliosis, thereby preventing future surgery? All of these things are what **really matter**. They are exactly why you're reading this book in the first place. You want to help your child be the

Breaking Through Special Needs

best version of themselves and as independent as they can be – always keep that at the forefront of your mind, that is, in your immediate consciousness. Allow them an opportunity to reach their potential. Remembering *that* will make it less difficult to find a few moments in the day during which you can incorporate a few exercises here and there.

With that in mind, let's get to the *why* of the exercises, shall we? I'm going to do this by referencing some frequently asked questions I get from parents visiting my clinic for the first time:

MUSCLE TONE VS. MUSCLE STRENGTH

"What is the difference between muscle tone and strength?"… you were asking yourself that exact thing, right?

Well, I've decided to put together a fact sheet for easy reference so that you, as a parent, can better understand your child. Knowing the difference goes a long way in piecing together the *why*.

Muscle **TONE** is defined as the tension in a muscle at rest. It is the muscle's response to an outside force, such as a stretch or change in direction. Appropriate muscle tone enables our bodies to quickly respond to a stretch. For example, if someone took your arm and quickly straightened your elbow, your biceps muscle would automatically respond and contract in response to protect you from injury.

A child with low tone, or **HYPOTONIA**, has muscles that are slower to react to a stretch and which are unable to sustain a prolonged muscle contraction. If a hypotonic child's arm was stretched quickly, the same way as mentioned above, there would be minimal to no response in their biceps muscle. Sometimes, the muscles of a child with low tone may feel soft and mushy or they may appear "floppy".

A child with high tone, or **HYPERTONIA**, has muscles that are in an "over-reactive" state, that is, in a state of high tension. If this child's arm was stretched, their biceps muscle would react even quicker and may maintain a prolonged contraction. In everyday movement there are constant stimuli, so this child may not be able to achieve relaxation of their muscles. Children with hypertonia are often at risk of a loss in range of motion and orthopedic issues.

Breaking Through Special Needs

MUSCLE STRENGTH is defined as the muscle's ability to contract and create force in response to resistance. Muscle strength is what your muscles exhibit when they aren't at rest. When you purposefully move a muscle, your brain is sending signals to your muscle fibers to contract. The power of your contraction is dependent upon your muscle mass; this can be changed by weight training and exercise. So, if an arm was stretched out, MUSCLE STRENGTH would be the ability to contract and actively resist that force.

In conclusion, although strength and tone are different, *when a muscle is not in an ideal position -meaning your child may have a tight muscle group (often seen with hypertonicity)- to be ready for contraction, muscle strength will be impaired.*

STRETCHING

I'll often suggest exercises or positioning that can help "reduce tone" or "break up tone" when it comes to our hypertonic (high tone) kiddies and adults. In contrast, I propose exercises and positioning to improve strength and alignment in our hypotonic (low tone) kiddies and adults. We see clients all along the spectrum of low to high tone, and we prescribe a bunch of different exercises to assist in helping them become more functional and independent. If we know the cause, we can help mitigate the problem.

Recently, I was having a conversation with a parent about stretching. Her son has Spastic Quadriplegic CP and his muscles are really tight pretty much everywhere, though his hamstrings (back of his thigh muscles) and adductors (inside thigh muscles) are particularly taught. Understandably, his mom wanted to know why his legs seem looser after PT, but then feel tight once again the following day. To demonstrate why this happens, I used a hair tie.

Over Time the Muscle Will Get Longer

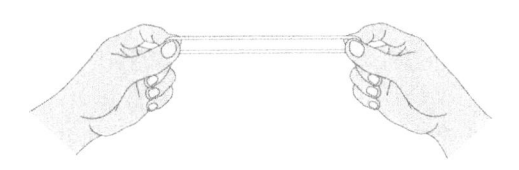

Breaking Through Special Needs

The black hair tie I used was brand new, so it was at its tightest at rest. I explained that, much like a muscle, when the hair tie is stretched, it can get way bigger, but once the stretching force (my hand) releases it, it goes back to normal. Over time, and if I repeat this action, the hair tie would gradually get more stretched out. With muscles, the principle remains the same, though it takes a lot longer since the stretching generally only happens in brief intervals.

As I explained to her, that doesn't mean that you should stop working on stretching the muscles: they will eventually get looser over time. The process definitely takes time and CONSISTENCY. One can also work on holding the stretch for a longer period of time: instead of just holding a stretch for a brief 15-30 seconds at a time, you can work on helping your child maintain a position for closer to a minute at a time and then work your way up. For this client, for example, holding a cross sitting position with a sand bag over his legs for 15-20 minutes was way more effective than just having him lay down and stretch his adductors for a few seconds. And the best part? We could even work on *reaching in sitting* while he held the stretch, thereby making the best use of the time! Consistently doing this means that his muscles will stretch out just like my hair tie – keep this in mind when you're stretching with your child.

That's just one quick example, but there are lots of different ways to increase the effectiveness of stretching. Another thing that's important to note is that following up stretching with mobility exercises is vital. Mobility exercises may mean getting them up into their equipment or helping them into another dynamic exercise to move their body I know that it might be hard to do, but strengthening the muscle right after stretching helps it to stay that way!

Babies with torticollis are good examples to illustrate this. Here at *Breakthrough*, we find many ways and opportunities for the babies to turn their heads in challenging directions… this is IN ADDITION to stretching and the execution of a range of motion activities. Challenging them to actively turn their head after stretching will help their positioning to correct over time!

Here's another thing to remember: stretching has to be done consistently and often. This is especially true for children/young adults who sit in

Breaking Through Special Needs

wheelchairs for most of the day. Stretching and mobility exercise HAS to be part of a routine. Doing exercises and stretches for one week will simply not make a significant impact. Doing a little, consistently, will eventually result in a positive impact. They will make big differences!

When it comes to stretching and mobility exercise, there is something very interesting that you may not have known. In individuals with neurological impairments, muscle tightness can actually stem from the brain. Did you know that? As the brain is the control center for the body, when it misfires, as it often does in special needs children, there is a disconnect between the brain and the body. In this case of someone with spasticity and high tone, for example, the brain automatically signals the muscles to become tight once again shortly after stretching. Therefore, consistent stretching is absolutely vital. Over time, muscle tightness turns in to a **contracture,** in other words, muscle tightness becomes irreversible: the lost muscle length cannot be stretched. This is exactly what we aim to avoid via the implementation of regular therapies and home exercise programs! For special needs children and adults, it's important to note that regular movement helps keep muscles loose.

Remember, stretching is important, but movement is even more so, as it forms a critical part of the day-to-day routine. Static stretching might not be enough to make meaningful change. Move and stretch your child consistently.

STRETCHING AND LOW TONE

I often hear the following from new parents: "my child is low tone, their muscles won't ever get too tight because they are already loose". This is FALSE. They may have lower tone in their muscles, but that does not mean they can't get tight muscles. I have treated so many clients who sit in adaptive seating all day because they need the support to sit, yet they have tight hip flexors and hamstrings that require a stretching and mobility routine despite their low muscle tone. *Just because they don't have normal resting tone, does not mean that having their muscles in a shortened range for prolonged periods of time won't make them tight.*

Breaking Through Special Needs

Tying it together

The most important aspect of a home exercise program or routine is that you can constantly ask for the advice of your team of therapists. This doesn't just go for physical therapy, by the way: it goes for occupational therapists and speech therapists, too. If you did just one thing from each service and combined it into all the areas of your daily routine, imagine how significant the leap towards your child's goals would be. How can you do that? Well, see if you can follow the guidelines below for inspiration:

1. Depending on what therapists you have for your child, know what goals they are currently working on, whether that be in school, home therapies, or outpatient centers.
2. Ask each provider the following: "How can I incorporate an exercise into my daily routine?"
3. Make sure their answers are actually things that you can do on a day-to-day basis, at home, in order to continue with your child's care outside of therapies.
4. Ask for a demonstration, if possible. If they are school therapists, ask for a video or picture so that you fully understand and your child will get the most out of it.
5. Find out from the therapists what time of day in YOUR normal routine is best suited to your child. Are the mobility routines and exercises best done before he/she gets out of bed in the morning, after bath time, or during lunch, etc.

Working things into your already hectic routine is no easy task – but please, trust me, it will most definitely be worth it. Lean on your team and make sure you're comfortable with the structure.

Stretching and mobility exercises are the single most crucial part of helping your child be the best that he/she can be. Remember the goal, keep the *why* at the forefront of your mind and stay consistent. I know you can do it.

If you're interested in our free home exercise guides for both stretching and mobility training, simply head to:
www.breakthroughptli.com/resources.

Lifting and Transfers

Let's take a minute to talk about lifting and transfers. To add to the incessant list of things you should be concerned about throughout the day, I know that having proper form and positioning for a transfer isn't always the top priority. However, I want to point out and remind you that the better you care for yourself, the better you can care for your child. So, that means if you have to continually lift and do transfers each day in some shape or form, it's important to be mindful of the way you're performing them. So, let's get into the details!

Have you ever injured yourself from a transfer with your child? Have you ever had difficulty with a child who is behavioral and won't get up or who you need to restrain? If your answer is yes, you wouldn't be the first one to say so. In fact, I speak with parents every single day about these challenges and how important it is for you, as the parent, to be able to keep up physically with these demands as your child gets older. Not only do I hear these stories, but I've lived through them, too. Yes, that's right! I may not have a special needs child of my own, but being a pediatric therapist means that I am constantly lifting and transferring clients all day long. Either that, or I'm repositioning them to help them perform a task. My body goes through its own wear and tear. That being said, even as a physical therapist myself, I've fallen victim to poor body mechanics and had injuries myself. Despite the fact that I get breaks from my work-routine!

My heart goes out to you. You as the parent don't get a break from the constant physical demands, so I really want to take this opportunity to guide you through what good body mechanics are really supposed to look like. I want to talk to you about how to manage behaviors, how to fall safely, and about my top tips for keeping you and your child safe. Apart from what you're about to read, please remember that I host live webinars and in person workshops on lifting and transfers to help guide parents – just like you – via demonstrations and examples. You're not alone. If you'd like to sign up for a replay, or to find out when our next one will be hosted, just go to: www.breakthroughptli.com/resources.

Breaking Through Special Needs

So, first things first. We often hear from parents that their biggest concerns center around their children getting taller and heavier and they know that they'll be unable to lift them properly. In other situations, the child may be ambulatory, but will just sit or lay down sometimes and, consequently, the parents are unable to get him/her back up. This can, of course, be distressing. Here at our clinic, we even hear of parents pulling out their necks or backs – injuries that can mean prolonged pain and frustration. Why? Because their child stiffened up into full extension and the parents were unsure of how to handle the situation. Navigating bathrooms, cars, and all of the other spots around the house, may prove difficult, because let's face it: our bodies were not made to lift as much – or as often – as you do in your daily routine. Unless that is, you're also a body builder with tons of free time to lift weights and hit the gym, and if that's the case, go YOU! But, that is not the typical presentation of parents I see and speak with every day.

If I had a dollar for every time I heard of a parent injuring themselves and/or tweaking their neck or back… I would have a whole lot of dollars! The thing is we, as humans, are not invincible. It's true, no matter how difficult it is to accept. And that's exactly why I want to dive into the details of how to keep you safe. You shouldn't have to deal with injuries related to lifting or transfers, and more often than not, you can't afford to be injured! Why? Because you're the one taking care of your child!

Here's a quick story before moving onto the really fun body mechanics and types of lifts:

We work with a family who has a 24 year old special needs child. She's fully dependent on her family for lifts, and she has spasms and constant movements that make it really tough for her to be helpful in any of the lifting. Her mom – a super woman by all standards – lifts her independently on a daily basis… to and from bed to her chair, her chair to the toilet, toilet to her chair, chair to her bed, etc. Would it ever be advisable to lift someone who's nearly 80 lbs. on your own? No. Absolutely not. Here's the thing, though… sometimes you don't have a choice, right? And in this case… I have to teach you a few things.

So one day, super-strong mom was lifting her daughter out of her adult stroller when she somehow got her foot wrapped around one of the leg

Breaking Through Special Needs

straps hanging down. She fell. She fell backwards while, of course, protecting her daughter; she saved her head from hitting the floor. At this point, super-strong mom is in extreme pain and can barely move, but do you know what her first instinct is? To grab her daughter a pillow off of the couch and to place it under her head. She literally dragged herself across the floor to reach for the pillow and place it under her daughter's head. Only then did she call for help. At the end of the day, mom found out she fractured her spine and had to stay in the hospital for a few days. She really is super woman.

This mother is the epitome all special needs parents: incredible strength, resilience, and love. You always put your child first… and in this case, even when you've fractured your spine! This bond is something so pure, and I love that about all of you parents. However, it can come at a cost sometimes… so, not educating yourself on how to take care of *you*, will detract from being the best parent you can be.

You know the first rule on planes, right? You're supposed to put your oxygen mask on before anyone else's. Well, the same principle applies in this situation. You need to learn to take care of your body so that you can continue to do the best for your special needs child.

Thankfully, when it comes to our super mom, there were no surgeries and there weren't any long term issues, but she still struggled: not having anyone around to really help her daughter while she was stuck in the hospital and unable to lift for months, was a really hard battle for her to face. I think you can relate to this feeling.

Accidents most definitely happen, and unfortunately their outcomes aren't always positive. By educating and teaching parents all around the world on lifts and transfers, these occurrences will hopefully get less and less, and parents will ultimately be able to continue to care for their children…. But ALSO keep THEIR own bodies safe.

Let's jump into how you can start doing this.

GENERAL BODY MECHANICS

SAFE BENDING

The best way to demonstrate this is through pictures or videos. Reading helps, but visual learning for something like this is incredibly valuable. That's why on our website, www.breakthroughptli.com, we have a spot in which you can sign up and get the replay of the "Lifting and Transfer Webinar". During this webinar, we educated parents across the US on proper body mechanics. What a day that was! If you're interested in watching, simply sign up here: www.breakthroughptli.com/resources. For now, though, I'll include pictures. Be sure to head to our *YouTube* page, though, simply by typing "Breakthrough Intensive Physical Therapy" into the search bar. There are many helpful videos for you there, too!

Let's get started!

Firstly, let's pretend we aren't lifting a human being for a moment. Do you think you know the correct way to lift? Even if you do, please read through and make sure you're hitting all of the points.

When it comes to safe bending, start with your feet shoulder width – or a little bit wider than shoulder width – apart. If you start with your feet close together, you leave yourself with a very narrow base of support. With a narrow base of support, you're more likely to fall or lose your balance, and ultimately you'll have less control of the rest of your body. Have a look below: I demonstrate this by using a nice, light beach ball.

Breaking Through Special Needs

Stance Don't!   Stance Do!

In order to pick up the beach ball, you have to make sure that you bend at your hips and knees, not your waist! Your back stays nice and straight as you pull your abdominals in and tighten your quadriceps and gluteal muscles. Pulling in your abdominals just means *tighten* them as if you're guarding yourself from someone hitting you in the stomach, without holding your breath. Tighten your quadriceps and/or hamstrings means the same thing. Activate those muscles on the upper part of your legs, front and back! In case you're unfamiliar, your gluteal muscles are those booty muscles. The more you activate your muscles, the better you protect yourself from injury. Your muscles will help stabilize your body. This is why it's extremely important to keep yourself healthy and strong if you're having to do this often.

We often go through the day not being aware of our mechanics and our body's methods of doing things until it hurts or something goes wrong. The stronger you keep your muscles on a day-to-day basis, the less risk you have of injuring yourself. Why? Because you'll be able to stabilize more… if you're using those strong muscles properly with good body mechanics!

Breaking Through Special Needs

Squat Don't!   Squat Do!

Here's a quick story to make you laugh.

One day, I was cleaning our office. It was only me in the office, as everyone else was off for the day. I decided that I needed to get into a crack between a piece of equipment and the wall because there was dog hair there from our therapy dog. So, the solution would've been to move the piece of equipment and then clean and put it back. The issue with this was, of course, that the piece of equipment I wanted to move was a six foot metal cage! Yet, because I was so determined and apparently thought I was the new "Hulk", I thought I could move this six foot metal cage independently. Ironically, this occurred after advising many parents that they shouldn't be lifting their older children independently! See, we all make mistakes, right!?

I'm certain that you can guess what happened next. Inevitably, I went to lift one side of the cage with proper leg form – of course – but because it's six feet high, I could not bend my waist properly. As I lifted, I immediately felt like my entire neck was out of place. I couldn't rotate or bend it in any direction! Luckily, there's a happy ending... I learned a big lesson after not being able to sleep for a few nights and having to do exercises/stretches on myself. I have to take care of myself! The point of my story? You can be "in-shape" and have good muscle strength, but if you're not practicing lifting properly, that is, with good mechanics, you are still at risk for injury.

Breaking Through Special Needs

And here's another tip: you always want to be as close to the object you are lifting as possible, even if that's just a small toy you're picking up from the floor.

Here's one last point on safe bending: if you have any physical restrictions, you can lower yourself to the floor safely by bringing yourself down to one knee (as pictured). To get back up from this position, it will require a little bit more core and leg strength, but it is a safe way to get yourself down to the floor to lift.

SAFE LIFTING

Now, let's get into the actual lifting part. As mentioned before, you need to get as close to your child as possible, and in this case, let's return to my beach ball. The further you are from whatever you're lifting, the worse off you are, as you can lose control more easily. You see, if you're lifting an object further away from you, the weight will be further away from your body, and that will not only make it harder for you to actually lift, but it will also put more strain on your body. So, to prevent your first potential problem, get as close to your child as possible!

Next, you want to be sure to "square up" to your child. I use that term because I used to play softball back in the day… and that's what sticks. But, in case you aren't sure what that refers to, I just mean: face your child. Try not to be at an angle to the side. This is important because you want to prevent any twisting as much as possible.

Ideally, you would always lift your child from a higher to lower surface. We all know "ideally" doesn't equate real life, though, right? Yet, higher to lower will always be easier, so just be mindful if you are lifting them from the floor to a chair, for example, or in any situation where it's lower to higher: you will have to use much more body strength than the alternative, and you'll need to be incredibly mindful of your mechanics and positioning.

Now, here's the tricky part. The body mechanics will be different for everyone, depending on how big your child is, how much they can assist you, and what kind of head and trunk control they have, etc. Despite this, I'll explain a few different methods I use to lift. Remember, all of the following are one person lifts. If you have a child that is older or much larger and/or heavier, you'll be using a two person lift – I'll go into this in just a moment. I want you to keep reading this part too, though, because I know you don't always have two people around. I know that a lot of it falls on one caregiver at a time, or in some instances, space can be so limited that only one person will be able to perform the lift.

First, you're going to lower yourself to wherever you're lifting your child from, whether it be the floor, bed, chair, whatever. Again, reminders:

1. You want to be as close to your child as possible.
2. Square up.

Using the perfect body mechanics that you just learned, you are either bending like a squat, or going down to one knee. Now, here's where it will depend on head/trunk control. If your child needs assistance in holding his/her head, you can support him/her with one arm under the neck/upper back so that the head will rest on your arm and prevent any unsafe extension. Your other hand can scoop under their pelvis.

Or…

If he/she has head and trunk control, you can sit him/her upright first, after which you can support their mid back and scoop under the thighs, close to the pelvis. Either way, you'll have to make the decision of which way works best for you and your child.

Breaking Through Special Needs

The most important next step is to lift them close your body first and then to stand up. This is such an important step and one that's rarely ever thought about. It goes back to the concept of getting them as close to your body as possible... before even starting the lift. You want them as central to your core, your center of balance, as possible. I realize this isn't always possible, but it is imperative that you at least try your best, or are at the very least be aware that/if he/she is further away from you than is ideal.

To stand, pull your child in close and then use your legs and buttocks to lift (without twisting). You want to make sure that you're using your legs as much as possible!

Often, if I'm lifting a client from the mat, I bend to a kneeling position, lift them onto my lap (as close as possible), and then, while maintaining a hold close to my center and core, I will use the half kneeling method to lift them back up. It also serves as a little rest break in case they're heavy or I need to reposition my hands or arms. If you'd like to see video examples of this, just head to **www.breakthroughptli.com/resources**.

TYPES OF LIFTS

Regardless of type of lift you need to use in order to transfer your child, it's important to note the set-up.

Let's imagine that we are transferring a child from his/her chair to the bed or vice versa. You want to have the position of surface to surface at a 45 degree angle. Even if you don't have a child who requires a wheelchair right now, yet you still need to perform transfers to and from the bath chair or assists from the floor, etc., then it's important for you, too. Often, if the lift is at 90 degrees – which is the most common error I see – you have to lift above the arm rests or sides of whatever they are seated in. If you just angle the lift to 45 degrees, then you're in a much better position to put less strain on your body and prevent twisting, too!

Quick tip: it's easier to transfer to your dominant side. If you're a righty, this just means the surface you're transferring your child to is on your right. Why? Because you may have to pivot or turn, and it's good to turn to your stronger side to do more of the work in that case.

Breaking Through Special Needs

Now that we've gotten that all covered... there are a multitude of different types and methods for lifting. I'm going to walk you through three of them and let you know in which situations you'll need them.

One Person Dependent Lift

This is when your child is small enough and light enough, but is unable to assist you in the transfer. Do you know what the weight limit for a one person dependent lift is? Well, maybe I've worded that wrong. In multiple school guidelines, the maximum weight for a one person dependent lift is just thirty five pounds. That means that any child over thirty five pounds should not be lifted independently; a two person lift, or a mechanical lift, should be used. Crazy right? While that may be the case, nearly every family I've worked with has broken this "rule"... including myself. I get it. Sometimes it's just not possible to have someone there with you, but it is important to keep the limit in mind.

That having been said, this one person dependent lift is exactly what I've explained in the section above. You either use a squat form, or you can try it from the half kneel position. It's incredibly important to remember to keep good body mechanics while performing this lift... and remember, depending on the child's head, neck, and trunk control, you'll know where to place your hands. If you are ever in doubt of whether you should be performing it independently or not, ask someone for help! It's always better to ask than to injure yourself.

Let's think about a scenario where your child is lying flat on his/her back. Do you think it would be easier to lift them from a sitting position or from a supine laying position? It actually comes down to preference, but if you can get them closer to your center of gravity (your trunk/main stabilizer), it will ultimately translate to a more secure lift. Typically, when he/she is lying flat, you need more upper body strength, but if they are sitting upright, then you can hug them into your trunk and it will be a more secure lift.

Two Person Dependent Lift

This type of lift should be used when your child is more than the ~35 lbs. threshold. Yes, thirty pounds seems light, but it's extremely important to protect yourself as much as possible, especially as a caregiver. Now, with

Breaking Through Special Needs

two people you could increase the risk for injury if you don't use good communication. There are two different types of two person transfers which can be employed to reduce this risk.

The one I recommend is the following:

One person takes the top half of the body and the other assists at the lower half/legs. For this transfer, one person has to lead the transfer. This should really be the physically stronger person between the two, and the one that does it most frequently. Whoever this leader is, he/she should be the person to take the top half of the child being transferred. They will also be the person to lead a count before the lift. Why? So that both people lifting will be able to lift *simultaneously* in order to prevent injury. The other person performing the lift will take the lower half.

Videos will be best for acclimatizing to this type of transfer, so head to our *YouTube* channel by typing in "Breakthrough Intensive Physical Therapy" and finding our videos on there!

The leader of the transfer will come alongside the child, widen his/her base of support, bend his/her knees, and grasp his/her arms under the child's arms. You want to make sure the arms are under their armpits because this is what will give you leverage and keep safety. It's almost like you're hugging them from behind (remember, keep them as close to you as possible). To make sure I have control when I perform these types of lifts, I usually grasp the forearms to maintain control of the child's arms and trunk as best I can. After grasping the child's forearms – when you actually perform the lift – you'll squeeze your arms together to assist in the lift, thereby making sure you don't injure yourself. By squeezing your arms together, it helps maintain the child's body close to yours, consequently keeping you both as safe as possible.

The other person will assist at the child's legs by scooping under his/her knees. Be sure to scoop your arms just above where their knees are (towards their hips). Why? Because, if you attempt to do so any lower, and the child's knees straighten out, you will lose your grasp and potentially cause the child to fall or someone to get hurt. Typically, the person assisting at the legs will either straddle the foot plates of the wheelchair, or wherever you are transferring from, and keep the child square to his/her body. Another option would be to assist from the side

Breaking Through Special Needs

in order to scoop the legs, but this technique doesn't allow you to maintain as much control over the actual lift.

What's important to remember, here, is that not every lifting situation is going to allow you to correctly square up your body or use proper body mechanics. You are going to have to find a situation that works best for you. One of the best examples I can share is a bathroom transfer. If you don't have an accessible bathroom then there is little to no way you'll be able to perform two person lifts with perfect mechanics – you can't fit two people in there at once!

When performing the lift, please remember your surface to surface angle of 45 degrees. The most important part of this transfer will be the count-off. Whoever the leader is will determine when each of you will lift the child, i.e. "on the count of three", or "one, two, three, up". Make sure you let your lifting counterpart know exactly when you plan to lift so that the timing can be simultaneous. If it is not, you may put yourself at risk for strain and injury, and we are all obviously trying to avoid that!

Another type of two person lift is a side by side lift. The reason I don't prefer this one is that is can be less safe and doesn't allow you to have as much control over the child or lift as you possibly can. I also don't prefer this one because a second of mistiming and it could potentially injure your child. That being said, it's still performed successfully and safely, and it does sometimes allow for better body mechanics, depending on the set up of the situation and transfer surfaces.

For this lift you still must have a leader who will do the count off, however, you will each be holding equivalent parts of the body. One arm will go underneath the child's arm and hold the forearm, and the other hand goes underneath the leg above the knee. *Kids with low tone, and who have less head and trunk control, are NOT the kids to do this transfer with.* Why? Because the child's shoulders could be strained on this type of lift and you could be placing them at risk of injury. Using proper body mechanics and proper communication for the count off, you ultimately lift the child by one arm and one leg each, thereafter turning to place them on the other surface. Again, watching a video example of this is probably best, so head to our *YouTube* channel now.

There you have it: two examples of two person dependent lifts that should be used when a child is too heavy to lift independently or if you are not confident in your ability to safely transfer the child!

Stand Pivot

To perform a lift like this, your child must be able to follow commands and have the ability to maintain weight bearing through his/her legs, albeit briefly and with assistance. Without that, this transfer wouldn't work. If it's possible to do this lift rather than a completely dependent lift, this is the best option for both you and your child. There's no weight limit for this lift either. Why? Because the child will really be supporting some of his/her weight, thereby allowing you to perform the transition. If he/she can't support enough of his/her weight for you to safely maneuver and assist, then performing it this way is not a good idea: you may then want to shift to a two person dependent lift.

For this lift, I'll use the example of moving a child from a chair to the bed. You'll want the bed on your dominant side, and you'll want to position the chair at about a forty five degree angle to the bed. Remembering good body mechanics, you square yourself to your child. You're going to bend your knees slightly – don't forget a wide base of support. Lean forward at your waist, keeping your back straight. Wrap your arms around the child's body… underneath their armpits, not around their neck. If they use you for support and are able to wrap their arms around you, then great, but be sure that their arms are not around your neck: you can injure your neck that way! To grasp around their trunk, I usually grab my right forearm with my left hand to secure the position.

From there, make sure you do a count off, because remember, the child should be able to follow commands. As the child pushes up to stand through their legs, you assist in the lifting and balance, and then pivot on your dominant – or more comfortable side – to sit them down. You really want to avoid twisting your trunk. Make sure you are pivoting on that dominant leg to whichever side you are transferring to! This one is pretty tough to just read, and you'll likely want to go see an example. So, if you do, head to our *YouTube* channel, "Breakthrough Intensive Physical Therapy", to get access to our videos!

HOW TO SAFELY FALL

And Voila! You've learned a few different transfer techniques. Those are the general guidelines, BUT we all know it doesn't happen like that. Typically, children stiffen using extensor tone, squirm, or just become dead weight. In lieu of this, falling is a super scary aspect to think about, but that's only because you don't know how to do it yet, or when it will happen, etc. Obviously, we try to avoid falling at all costs, but that doesn't mean accidents don't happen. The goal of the next few tips are to prevent a fall in so far as possible, but also how to allow yourself to fall safely should the need arise.

Here are three things that I teach parents all of the time:

1. **Awareness**
   Scan your environment! What if you were to fall... where would you need to go? Before lifting, especially if you are by yourself, pay close attention to your environment. Scan what's around you and make sure that there aren't things lying around. Maybe there are toys on the floor or a pillow from the couch... maybe there's a rug on top of hardwood flooring and your foot is placed on the edge, thereby presenting a tripping hazard. Whatever it may be, you have to scan your environment first. All too often, I hear about how rushed parents feel all of the time, yet I am certain you wouldn't regret an extra 30 seconds of scanning the environment if it meant you wouldn't fall during a transfer you were performing.

2. **Positioning**
   Theirs AND yours! Do you have enough room to bend your legs properly? Do you have to scoot your child forward in his/her chair beforehand in order to gain a better position for yourself? If you can't get yourself in a position to have good body mechanics, what do you need to change? What areas of your body should you tighten up if you can't bend your legs appropriately?

3. **Your plan**
   If you are by yourself, how will you turn your body, and where are you transferring your child safely to? Don't forget, you want the surface you're transferring him/her to, to be as close as possible to prevent injury. If you are doing a two person lift, have you designated

who is leading and counting off? Explaining thoroughly what you are about to do, and confirming with the other person that he/she is ready and has a good hold, is imperative. Don't forget, it's easier to go from higher to lower surfaces, if possible.

If you just think about these three things, you're already in a better position to perform a safe transfer. It will take time to get into new habits, but if you do it, you'll absolutely be in a better position to perform a safe transfer and lift for yourself and for your child. It's most definitely a habit worth honing.

What do you do when they don't act like perfect angels while you lift them?

If you find yourself in a tough situation, what do you do? What if they stiffen up? What if they push themselves as stiff as boards, or grab you as you're trying to lift? This is obviously very realistic, and you all face these situations daily. Hopefully, you've already planned and observed your environment, but if not, you must try to slow the fall, NOT stop it. You are at a higher risk of injury trying to prevent the fall than if you were to attempt to control it to the floor. Obviously, this is much harder when you are carrying someone independently, but you must at least try to find a spot. If it is that your child is stiffening up, check his/her head positioning and make sure it is not in extension. If it is an extension, it can trigger tone. If the chin comes down, you can relax his/her body a little more in order to safely place them where you need to.

GUIDELINES OF WHEN TO USE A LIFT

Like I mentioned earlier, typical school guidelines for safe lifting is 35 pounds. I know that sounds like an extremely low number, but my guess is that they wouldn't make a recommendation if it wasn't in their best interest. They obviously don't want any of their staff members getting hurt! Now, I do realize that this number is probably unrealistic for many of you, and you likely need to continue to do one person lifts for someone double that weight... or sometimes even heavier. But, when that's the case it is even more essential for you to be aware of your environment, set up your plan, and make sure you are always doing your best to utilize proper body mechanics!

Breaking Through Special Needs

My last little tip on this is to go with your gut. If you're feeling unsure and can ask another person for help, absolutely do so. If you're unsure and don't have someone around, yet you need to perform the transfer or lift anyway, set yourself up for success by following the proper positioning of surface to surface, proper body mechanics, and of course, have a contingency plan if things don't work out as planned.

EXERCISES TO HELP KEEP YOU STRONG

This chapter wouldn't be complete without giving you tools and strategies to prevent injuries and for keeping your bodies strong for the increased demands placed on them. I'll give you a simple set of exercises that can – and should – be worked into your daily routine, not only if you feel you tweaked something or pulled a muscle! To reiterate, a general strengthening program is recommended so that you can continue to perform lifting and transfers properly and with more ease. Unfortunately, there aren't always others to be able to help you, so hopefully these exercises and stretches serve as a good starting point for you to learn to take care of your body to be your best self for your child.

Standing Extensions

For this exercise, you'll begin in a standing, upright position, with your hands resting on your hips. Slowly arch your trunk backwards and hold for 3 seconds. Repeat this 10x daily. Make sure to maintain your balance during the exercise and do not bend your knees.

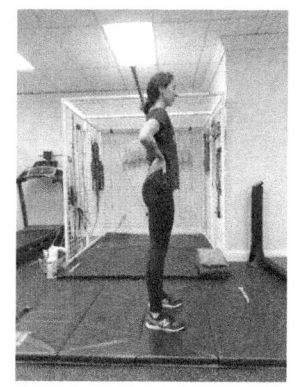

Starting Position   Extension Position

Prone Press Ups

Breaking Through Special Needs

For this exercise, you'll be on the floor… so, grab your mat if you need one. Begin by lying on your stomach and resting on your elbows low to the ground. Push up on your elbows, bending your back upward. Make sure to keep your hips in contact with the floor, and maintain a gentle chin tuck throughout the exercise. You can hold this one for 5 seconds and perform 10 of them, daily of course.

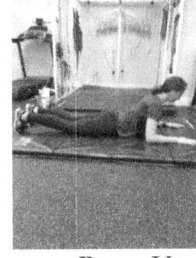

Starting Position　　　Press Up　　　Challenge!

Child's Pose with Side Bending

Begin on all fours. Sit your hips back onto your heels and hold. Then, reach your hands forward and to the side as you continue to sink further into the stretch. Repeat on both sides. This is my absolute favorite stretch of all time! Hold at least 20 seconds and do it 2-3 times.

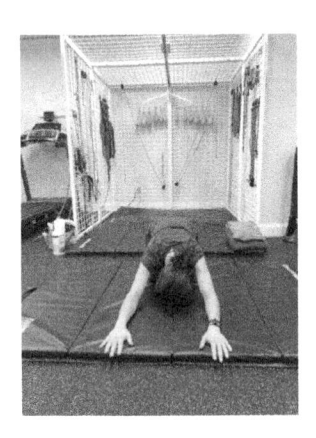

Breaking Through Special Needs

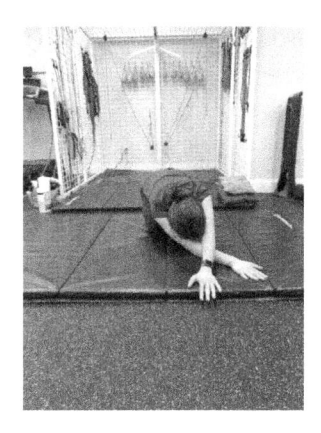

Supine Core Activation

Begin by lying on your back with your knees bent and feet resting on the floor. You're going to draw in your abdominals as if you are pulling your belly button to the floor. Hold, then relax... and repeat. Make sure to keep your back flat against the floor and avoid performing a sit up motion. Hold for 2 seconds and then repeat 10x.

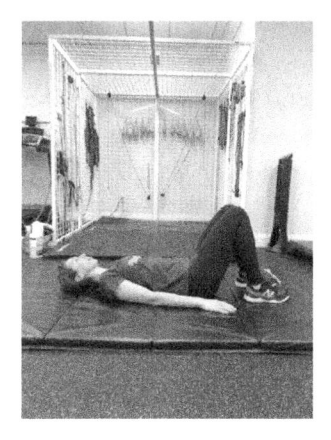

Bridges

Begin by lying on your back with your arms lying straight out to your sides, your legs bent at the knees, and your feet flat on the ground. You're going to tighten your abdominals and slowly lift your hips off of the floor into a bridge position, keeping your back straight. Make sure to keep your trunk tight throughout the exercise and your arms flat on the floor. Hold upwards in the bridge for 5 seconds and repeat 10x.

Breaking Through Special Needs

Straight Leg Raise

Begin by lying on your back with your legs straight. Take a gentle breath in. As you exhale, tighten your abdominal muscles and lift one leg a few inches off of the ground. Hold, and then lower it back to the ground and repeat. If you feel strain on your back during this, it means you need some core work. Following this, you can bend your opposite knee in, with your foot flat, to accommodate and prevent your lower back from arching too much. Avoid pushing out your abdomen as you raise your leg!

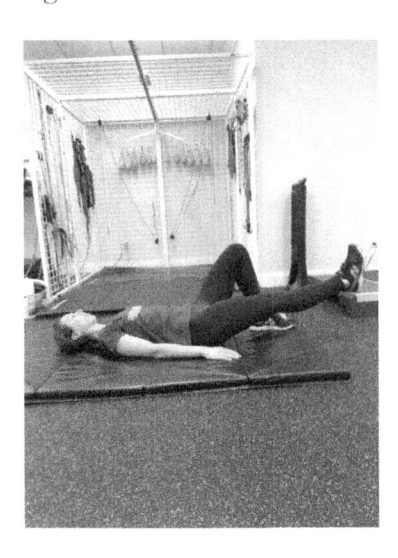

Breaking Through Special Needs

If you'd like a handout guide that you can print and keep with you or put on the fridge, head to www.breakthroughptli.com/resources now!

These are all exercises that will help you stretch your back and exercise your core, both of which are essential for healthy and safe lifting. Although they are basic, they shouldn't be disregarded. Adding these to a strengthening routine will enhance your body's mechanics, and you will ultimately be able to stay strong and healthy for the physical demands you face each and every day.

Hopefully you've been able to learn something from this information. Even if it just helps you to think about what your positioning is, how it can be easier, and what you need to do to do it safely, then I've succeeded. Being a parent of someone with special needs means you have a lot of unexpected tasks to do. Set yourself up for success so that you can continue to be the best version of yourself for your family. Don't forget to access your resources, here: www.breakthroughptli.com/resources!

Alternative Therapies

Lifting and transfers done, let's turn to something a little different: alternative therapies.

Some of you may know of many alternative therapies already, but equally, many of you may not. Researching things takes time, and I know that time isn't something you have much of. Special needs children are always involved in therapies, whether it be behavior therapies, physical therapy, occupational therapy, speech therapy, or vision therapy, etc. So, you might be thinking what other therapies even exist, and when would you ever have time to pursue them? I totally get it, but educating yourself about certain things is never something you'd regret, and if anything, it just opens your mind to what possibilities are out there are for your child... and then you get to choose the direction you go in.

Sometimes, trying the same things over and over simply doesn't not work. Have you ever had a therapist who kept working on one way of helping your child achieve a task, yet your child wasn't responding well? Maybe it was the way it was being taught, or maybe it was the activity itself, but constantly **adjusting and using various methods of teaching** is imperative for helping children. Alternative therapies could improve your child's quality of life in a different way... just when you thought you may have exhausted all of your options. Whether it is simply getting into the pool for the first time, attempting standing on his/her own, or simply trying new activities, the following alternative therapies could be the gateway to new – and more – progress!

INTENSIVE THERAPY

I'll obviously have to highlight one of my personal favorites – which we actually perform in my facility! I always say that I don't always recommend certain therapies or techniques for every child, and I absolutely don't think the way we do things at our facilities are the only way to get progress and make new gains, but what I can tell you is that I've seen intensive therapy work... time and time again. Each and every child we've seen and been able to help has made improvements in some way; they have worked towards their goals no matter how big or small they may be. I've seen children and adults at many different levels of abilities, and I've continually seen progress towards becoming more independent, stronger, and more confident.

Intensive therapy utilizes the TheraSuit® method. This intensive therapy method of treatment sticks to a strict regime: working 3 hours per day, for 5 days per week, 3-4 weeks at a time. At our facility, we offer modified programs, too, as a supplement to school and home PT, and guess what... *it still works*. I'll tell you why.

This type of therapy utilizes specialized equipment, thereby eliciting different outcomes. I mean, of course, the Universal Exercise Unit and the TheraSuit itself. The TheraSuit is considered a soft, dynamic orthosis that the child or adult wears during his/her therapy sessions. It can look a little crazy sometimes, especially if you've never seen it before, but it provides a significant amount of sensory input into the muscles and helps align the child to the proper positioning in order to perform their work. It supports and challenges him/her as he/she performs different types of activities. It even has leg pieces that can help facilitate a normal walking pattern. So, performing high repetitions of functional activities while wearing this drastically improves the outcome.

Alongside the TheraSuit is the Universal Exercise Unit. I call this "the cage", but sometimes parents get intimidated by that phrasing (before they really get to know me), so let's be politically correct and say Universal Exercise Unit. As a side note, I once had a parent ask me to call it a "fun cube", so it was a "fun cube" for some time. It's hard to grasp the concept just by reading these words, so I've put together some resources for you on to check out in case you're more curious about how the equipment works. Simply head to www.breakthroughptli.com/resources for these.

The 'fun cube' has bungees that attach to a belt inside of it, all of which serve as a harness support system. The bungees provide weight and balance assistance for children and adults. This is essential in helping them achieve functional positions, tasks, and transitions, etc. that they would normally not be able to do without the assistance. The best part of the 'fun cube' is that because of the bungees supporting the child/adult, the PT can likely remove a lot of additional support that the client would normally have needed in order to achieve a position or task. In other words, the child/adult gets to feel what it's like to stand or sit "by themselves".

For example, we see a 22 year old with Spastic Quadriplegic Cerebral Palsy on a regular basis. Before coming to our facility, he had very limited stance time, no longer had school therapies, and drove around in a power wheelchair as his primary means of mobility. In the Universal Exercise Unit, he gets to feel what it's like to stand independently without hands and support... *and he loves it!* Because of that, he's learned how to walk with a posterior rolling walker for up to 15 -20 steps! I will repeat... he's done this even at the age of 22! You can read about his success story in my "Feel Good Stories" chapter towards the end of this book.

Here's another example involving another of our clients, albeit that he is at a slightly higher level. He is diagnosed with Autism and can walk, run, and transition, but still presents with weaknesses that limit his ability to be truly independent. After some time working with this equipment and skilled therapists, he is able to perform floor to stand transitions without the use of his arms! Practicing with the bungees allowed him to feel independent, gain balance, and, over time, gain the strength needed to perform this activity all by himself. Amazing, right? This really works! Sure, there are precautions in certain cases, but in these situations, we would never suggest it.

We provide full intensive programs, but many of our clients are seen 1-2 times weekly and still make incredible progress towards their goals. I know I mentioned it earlier in this book, but you know those school and home therapy sessions that only last *a half an hour* at a time? That length of a session is extremely challenging... I speak from experience of also having been a school PT. Why? Because these kids need more repetitions to make meaningful gains. They need more, but Medicaid and school districts don't want to pay for it and they often try to cut services before they should be cut. This is why seeking alternative intensive therapy is essential to helping children reach their goals. Now, don't get me wrong, there are many districts that are fair in their service distribution, however there's been too many times that I've seen it unfairly distributed, and that's when it is no longer in the best interest of the child and their goals. *It turns into what is best for the school district and their budget.*

Breaking Through Special Needs

Thirty minute sessions just aren't enough to make meaningful gains. At our facility, we don't see clients for less than one hour at a time. Children with neurological diagnoses require thousands more repetitions to achieve a functional task. Imagine that it takes us 10,000 repetitions to learn how to crawl, but a child with a neurological diagnosis may need 100,000 repetitions to be able to learn. Why? Because their brains need to create new pathways of learning. So, a full intensive program of three hours per day, for five days per week, for three weeks, SEEMS like it might be crazy, yet it is where we see the most rapid progression of skills and development. One of the best parts is that as the children advance gross motor skills, they often improve in their speech and language development, too. They learn to support their core and breathing better, and they learn to move their bodies in ways that they haven't before. If you'd like to hear more stories of the children we've been able to help, skip to the last chapter and read some more feel good stories. Just come back when you're done!

Hippotherapy

There are probably many of you who have heard of this, and maybe even have your children involved in a program, but I want to mention it for those who might not know about it or its benefits. Hippotherapy is just equine assisted therapy. It can also be considered therapeutic horseback riding. It is used widely within the special needs population across many different levels and abilities. As with anything, there are precautions, but in general it offers many benefits to those who do qualify.

Hippotherapy is used to improve muscle tone, mobility, and core strength/posture. It involves horseback riding and channeling a horse's natural movement to improve posture over time. The core exerts patterns of movement and rhythm as the horse walks/trots, thereby forcing the rider's trunk to mimic this movement, resultantly influencing proper alignment. Over time, this can help while off of the horse too!

In one study, specifically for children with Cerebral Palsy, hippotherapy was performed twice weekly for 6-12 weeks. Over that time, there were significant improvements in gross motor function, sitting balance, speed of walking, length of stride, and postural alignment. Gains were noted in the balance of their heads and trunks, which ultimately contributes to an improved quality of life and independence during daily activities (Martin-

Valero, 2018). If hippotherapy is offered near you, it is most definitely worth a shot. It may well be another tool in your toolbox for helping you get the most out of your child in order to help them reach their full potential.

Aquatic Therapy

Aquatic therapy is an alternative therapy option for any child or adult with mobility limitations. It is water based exercise that assists in reducing pressure on muscles, bones, and joints, and it encourages free movement. A child may be able to perform exercises or movements that they are unable to perform on land. This is due to the effect of the water has on the body, as it offers buoyancy. It can aid in improving flexibility, strength, and endurance for improved mobility. The concept of water buoyancy reducing the weight of gravity is very similar to the concept of weight assist for bungees in the Universal Exercise Unit. Though different, both strategies take weight away from the individual so as to be able to perform tasks he/she normally wouldn't be able to perform.

Something you may not know is that, although the buoyancy is able to reduce the weight of gravity, there are also compressive forces underneath the water. This is called "hydrostatic pressure". The deeper you go, the stronger these forces are. The fact that this pressure exists means that, if your child is working in the pool and their trunk is underwater, the hydrostatic pressure applies a constant resistance to the chest wall. When you inhale (breathe in), the chest wall expands. When you breathe out, the chest wall compresses. So, in the water, the hydrostatic pressure applies constant resistance during the entire movement and creates positive results! It can force us to release more air than we would normally exhale and it can help the chest wall work more efficiently with carryover effects outside of the water (Kawadler, 2016).

Aquatic therapy can also help improve circulation. As some of you may know, circulation can be limited due to increased time spent in a wheelchair or seated position. So, when a child actually stands, their feet turn red because blood flow rushes to that area more than it typically does. Having the hydrostatic pressure of the water on his/her legs, assists in full circulation of blood flow throughout the limbs and body.

Overall, aquatic therapy is a great option for many children with special needs no matter how high or low their physical level may be.

Music Therapy

Research articles are likely not needed for this section. Throughout my career as a pediatric therapist, one thing I can say for certain is that, amongst nearly all of the children and adults I have worked with, their responses to certain types of music and music therapy is incredible. There is not "one kind" of music that works better than others; it all comes down to individual preferences and needs. Music therapy uses sound and rhythm to enhance cognitive function, speech, and motor skills. Whether the music therapist assists the child in making music or just encourages listening, it can improve auditory responses, language processing, relaxation, and communication skills. The beat of the music can help the brain form meaningful connections related to concentration and focus. It is a fun and interactive therapy which assists in enhancing cognitive functioning as well as alertness.

A study, performed for children in Early Intervention services who were either visually impaired, autistic, physically impaired, and/or speech impaired, indicates my point clearly. The individuals received music therapy only twice each, for 30 minute sessions at a time. The results demonstrate that the children were on task throughout both 30 minute sessions, and when observed in peer interactions, they were able to interact with others more effectively. So, not only did it help them focus and pay attention, it also helped them in their socialization skills too. Music therapy may not be the first thing you think of when trying to find therapies to help your child be the best version of themselves, but it is most definitely an outlet that is proven effective and beneficial for special needs children and adults (Standley, 1996).

Overall, the point of demonstrating how alternative therapies work is to prove to you that you are not bound to the therapies you currently have. Even if you may not have the above services directly accessible to you in your area, the internet is a wonderful tool to use. Virtual services may be available (maybe aside from the pool), and it is most definitely worth at least looking into if you're keen to have your child reach their full potential. Give it a go, and visit **www.breakthroughptli.com/resources** for more tips, information, and advice!

The Legalities... From Someone Who Isn't A Lawyer

There are so many beautiful joys that come with having a special needs child, but there are also many unique challenges you face as a parent. Unfortunately, you're seldom prepared for these. Let me preface this chapter by reiterating that I am not a lawyer. I am simply a business owner and physical therapist who has seen so many parents struggle with confusing issues, without ever really having any direction or guidance. So, this section of my book is to give you some general information, even though it may be difficult to face.

I can't tell you how many times a parent has explained that their worst nightmare is their child outliving them. There are so many unknowns, and how can you ever truly prepare for something like that? Nobody wants to think about it, and it could possibly be one of the scariest aspects of raising a child with special needs. As your child gets older, you realize that you won't be around forever, and you have to prepare for when you aren't... but, how do you do that? Nobody has created a manual (that I know of), and so I want to include some facts and resources, in here, for you to read through in order to make this daunting task more manageable. Maybe you've already done a lot of what I'm about to go through, maybe you haven't and need to, or maybe your child is so young that you feel you're not at that point yet. I understand that, but when it comes to your child's future, you can never be too early. It's important to shield yourself with facts and education on the topics of guardianship and trusts. Why? So that you can prepare for quite possibly the one thing you want to think about least.

Guardianship

Guardianship is not necessary in every case, and it is something you can't necessarily do before your child turns 18, yet it is still beneficial to educate yourself on the facts and what you will need to do should the day arrive. I say this because I once worked with a family who wasn't aware

Breaking Through Special Needs

that they needed to do this – their son was 20 years old and very fragile. Their son had no capacity to make financial or medical decisions independently, yet because there was no guardianship over him, if anything were to happen, the parents would not retain the right to make the decisions for him. Thankfully, they were able to immediately seek assistance and to navigate this with no incidents occurring, but what a scary thought that they would not have had a say in their son's care if *something did*.

Guardianship is necessary for children and young adults that do not have the ability to make their own medical decisions. You have to do some paperwork, and either you as the parent can be appointed by the court to have guardianship, or another family member can. To do this, though, there needs to be documentation that your child cannot make informed medical or financial decisions independently, and a psychological evaluation must be made. To help prepare yourself for this as your child nears the age of 18, research who you may want him/her to go to for this evaluation: have a list handy.

Different states may require different documentation, and the process may vary, so I won't even bore you with the details of how it works. However, prepare yourself for this – it would be best to speak to an attorney who directly handles special needs cases in your area. Go to someone you can meet in person so that you can develop a relationship with them, as they will be helping you navigate a not-so-easy task, and so that they can be part of your team.

SPECIAL NEEDS TRUSTS

Setting up a trust can be tricky. Why? Because you obviously want to maximize your child's benefit when it comes to the resources they receive, yet there are complications when your child receives Medicaid or Security Supplemental Income (SSI). We've had attorneys and financial planners come in to host workshops for us, all of whom specifically work with special needs families and, all too often, parents are surprised by their advice. The typical, "have a bank account in their name and put money from birthdays, events, other family in there" that parents responsibly set up when they have a child, could actually be putting the child at risk. How? Well, because it's in their name, they may not receive certain benefits.

So, the goal of setting up a special needs trust is to set your child up for success financially, that is, without any sort of disqualification from government assistance. These children and adults deserve so much and are underserved already: setting up a trust that will care for them financially is essential.

I'd like to describe two types of special needs trusts, but again I'd like to reiterate that seeking an attorney and financial advisor who has experience in setting these up is your best course of action.

One type of trust is a **first party trust.** This is typically used when the child or adult receives inheritance or a court-mandated settlement. With this type of trust, if the child or adult passes, the remaining assets are used to reimburse the state for Medicaid benefits used during his/her lifetime. On the other hand, a **third party trust** is the most common. These are funded by other parties aside from the child/adult beneficiary. This means that you as the parent can fund this account and have a separate person as the "trustee" who manages it. With this type of trust, then, there can be multiple beneficiaries, which can ultimately be a useful planning tool. There is a ton more information out there about trust, how much to fund the accounts, and how to best use government assistance programs, however, I am not the person from whom to seek guidance about that. Your best bet would be to research local attorneys in your area who, again, are familiar in setting these up, then go from there.

***

The one thing that comes up with setting up guardianship and trusts for your child is that it is incredibly hard for parents: you are planning who will care for your child when you are gone. So many parents have told me how they wrestled with their decisions because they feel it's too early to put them in the care of their siblings, or they don't feel it's fair to place the weight and responsibility on their other child(ren). It's the last thing you really want to think about and it's scary. I understand that. It's scary to think about your child's life without you in it, because from day one you've grown accustomed to providing everything for him/her; picturing someone else having to do all of the tasks you do – with the same amount of care and love – seems impossible.

Breaking Through Special Needs

I will tell you what one special needs parent told me a long time ago. She explained that she kept a journal for "just in case" purposes. It was a journal of all of the things that aren't included in his/her medical history, but make your child who he/she is. She would write down when her daughter feels cranky, or that, if you tickle under her belly button, she'll smile; she wrote down that her daughter loves reading books before bed, but that you have to skip to the end in certain books because she loves the illustrations. In other words, she wrote down all the things that nobody told her to write.

So, yes: you can have a close family member who takes care of your child, but they won't know all of the little things you, as their parent, do every single day; they won't know those things that fill your child's day with love and helps him/her get the best quality of life. When it came to the mom I just mentioned, she continued to write. As her daughter grew up and got older, she just continued to journal all of her daughter's likes, dislikes, how to cheer her up, and what she loves to do each morning and night, etc. What an incredible resource that would be should anything ever happen, right?

Even though these things are scary, hard, and uneasy to think about, if there's anything to take from your experience as a parent of a child with special needs, it is that life may go very differently to how you originally intended it to be. Set yourself up for success by navigating these topics as soon as possible. Do so with professionals who will be another part of your trusted team.

Clinical FAQ's...

SHOULD MY CHILD GET BOTOX?

While I cannot provide you with a definite answer, I *can* give you a little information to help you make the best decision. If you have a child with special needs who has spasticity and tightness, you are most likely very familiar with Botox injections. For those of you who aren't, though, here is a little background:

Botox is a drug that is injected into hypertonic and spastic muscles in order to weaken the signal via blocking the connections between the nerves and the muscles. It is typically said to last 3-6 months... if it has an effect on your child.

While reducing spasticity and high tone can be great, there are always other factors to look at. Sometimes, when a person has lived with high tone for longer periods of time – whether it be from birth or after an accident/stroke – he/she actually learns to use the high tone in order to benefit himself/herself functionally. For example, a child who has difficulty rolling from their back to their belly can use the high tone in their arm muscles to assist in the functional movement which is, in this case, rolling. If this same child was to get Botox injections in his/her arm muscles, the weakness of those muscles will become evident; the child will then have difficulty rolling because this/her muscles are not strong enough to perform the same task. Now, this is definitely not always the case... but, it can be.

Additionally, after Botox injections it is very important that the child has a routine in place for stretching and strengthening. Why? Well, so that he/she is able to prolong the effects of the Botox. However, as I mentioned, the effects do not last. Botox can, however, be extremely beneficial if the child is able to gain a range of motion or strength in the injected muscles.

Let me say this, though: every single person is different. Issues or problems associated with the neurological system are never exactly the same between people, and while it may work for some, it may not work for others.

A shortened answer:

Botox *may* work for your child. Again, effects typically last 3-6 months at a time if your child has a positive response. If you are interested in this route for your loved one, it is always best to get more than one doctor's opinion before trying any new drugs.

A longer answer:

Try an alternative therapy. Alternative therapy options help your child reduce tone *and* strengthen in a natural way, all without adding more medications and injecting your child with something that may or may not work. Companies themselves have said that Botox should not replace any existing physical therapy routines. And, as with any drug given, there are side effects and risks. There are ways to help reduce tone, naturally, without enduring injections or adding another medication to the list.

What is body awareness?

I constantly have an ongoing discussion with parents… especially in evaluations when describing what I'm observing in their child's movement patterns and mobility in the environment. I was recently describing what the term, "body awareness" meant to a parent after noticing her hypotonic/"low tone" daughter was stumbling when trying to walk around and navigate the gym environment.

So, what is body awareness, really?

Body awareness is the internal understanding of where your body is in space. It relies on "proprioceptive input", A.K.A, sensory information from your muscles and joints going to your brain.

Here's an example of what I mean: I hold my arm out to the side of my body. Now, I close my eyes and still know that my arm is out to the side. At this moment, I know where my arm is in space… in relation to the rest of my body. This is really important when orienting one's body to the surrounding environment and navigating it. Being aware of our body's position is something that happens automatically and naturally. In other words, the proprioceptive sense allows us to position our bodies

Breaking Through Special Needs

just so in order to enable our hands, eyes, ears, and other parts to perform actions or jobs at any given moment.

This awareness allows us to walk around objects in our path, to move a spoon to our mouths without looking at the spoon, and to stand far enough away from others while waiting in a line at the grocery store. It enables a student to write without pressing too hard or too lightly on their pencil, and it helps us to brush our hair with just the right amount of pressure.

WHAT DOES A LACK OF PROPRIOCEPTION/BODY AWARENESS LOOK LIKE?

- Difficulty learning new movements, ESPECIALLY if that movement is a gross motor task. When a child with poor body awareness tries mimicking a movement or task, it is more challenging. Why? Because he/she has a harder time understanding where his/her body parts are, as well as how much to move them in order to mimic the movement.

- Clumsy, uncoordinated: people with poor body awareness will appear clumsy or uncoordinated. They may not realize how close their foot is to an object while walking, because they have a harder time knowing where their feet really are.

- Don't like the dark or closing their eyes. These children rely heavily on vision for feedback because of their poor ability to know where they are in space. So, taking away their major feedback source by closing their eyes or placing them in the dark, makes it more challenging for them.

WHAT CAN YOU DO ABOUT IT?

If you've heard your child's therapist speak about this term before, and you've not quite known what it means, then hopefully this helped! If you notice some of the things mentioned above, but haven't related it to poor body awareness... it's okay! Here are a few things you can try at home to help your child:

- Pushing/pulling weighted objects: laundry basket with heavier objects inside it to weigh it down.

Breaking Through Special Needs

- Jumping on a trampoline.
- Lifting and carrying weighted objects: a weighted ball if you have it, or books.

If your child isn't as mobile, you can try applying some deep pressure to their arms and legs.

What is causing my child's balance problems?

We see and hear reports of balance issues a lot… whether your child has difficulty navigating throughout the community, or just has a hard time standing in one place by themselves, balance is HUGELY important. In fact, balance plays a large role in his/her ability to perform daily tasks independently.

Here are five reasons why your child may have poor balance, as well as the tell-tale signs.

1: Visual Impairment:

Sure, it may seem as though your child is just weak and doesn't want to listen to you, but a reason that they have poor balance could be poor visual efficiency. Your eyes give your brain a lot of feedback, particularly about where you are in space. Please note, this doesn't mean *clarity* of vision, although that could also be a contributing factor. Visual efficiency is actually how well our eyes interpret our environment in order to see one, clear image. If our eyes don't synchronize with what's around us, it could most definitely be causing balance impairments!

2: Decreased Core Strength:

It always comes back to core stability. If we have a weak core, it throws off the balance of the rest of our bodies. We're likely to think that leg and hip weakness is the culprit – which it can be, a lot of the time – but, it must always start at the core. You can have really strong legs, but if you can't stabilize your trunk, then you won't be able to stand still or maintain your balance. Even if your child isn't quite standing yet, he/she may not be able to hold their head upright due to inadequate core strength.

Breaking Through Special Needs

3: Poor Body Awareness:

You should know this term now from reading the above, but in case you haven't, it simply refers to your ability to know where your body is in space. For example, if I hold my arm out to the side, my brain knows that I am holding my arm out to the side: my brain gets feedback which tells me that. Sometimes, however, if that processing is a little off, we don't get quality feedback to tell us where our body is, so that can therefore contribute to a lack of coordination and even safety.

4: Poor Midline Development:

Similar to the concept above, it is really important to know where our middle is. It helps us stay upright and stay centered. If your child doesn't have a true sense of their midline, he/she will have difficulty balancing and keeping a good posture.

5: Reflex Integration:

Fancy words, but not too complicated. We are born with reflexes. As we grow, these reflexes integrate, meaning they go away and are no longer present. We requite them only as infants. With neurological conditions, these reflexes may not integrate.

Let's use the Babinski reflex as an example. This reflex normally doesn't present after the age of 2, and it can affect balance. The Babinski reflex occurs when, after the sole of the foot has been firmly stroked, the big toe moves toward while the top surface of the foot, as well as the other toes, fan out. This movement is triggered by a nerve path which starts at our feet and goes all the way up to our cortex and back down our body. When children retain the Babinski reflex for too long, it means they don't have a clear central nervous system and their brain has to work harder on other functions. A child who retains the Babinski reflex will find it uncomfortable to put their feet on the floor and will not have good balance. Why? Because their toes and the inside of their foot arches will always want to come up off of the floor. This is a common, normal reaction for babies before the age of two, but imagine if your feet could not touch the floor without wanting to come up off of it!

Breaking Through Special Needs

There are many more reasons why your child's balance could be off, and it may be even be a result of a combination of factors. The above 5 reasons are a good place to start, though. What's most important is that you are aware of the fact that issues like this affect the quality of not only your child's life, but also your family's life as a whole.

Why is walking down the steps harder?

Typically, when you see that it's difficult for your child to step down steps – which is common, by the way – it's due to one of two really common reasons:

1. Limited Range of Motion in The Leg

An example of this is if a child has a lack of range of motion and mobility in their ankle joint, that is, difficulty in moving his/her toes up/down: pressing down the gas pedal, lifting the foot off of the gas pedal. This is could be due to either surgery or contractures.

As a side note, ankle orthotics could also cause this compensatory movement pattern. Depending on which type of orthotics the child may have, it could limit the range in his/her ankle to move up or down, thereby causing a different navigation pattern. For example, if your child has SOLID AFOs, meaning there is no hinge or movement at the ankle joint, this completely limits the child's ability to move this/her ankle and to adjust to different positions. Having trouble picturing it? Well, imagine your ankle was fixed at a 90 degree angle and you couldn't move it up or down. Now, imagine stepping down with the other leg – what compensations do you notice? In the same way, then, the child might have difficulty leaning forward or bending his/her knee, solely because it's a blocked movement for his/her ankle.

For those same reasons, you see compensatory strategies without braces, though they may have different causes, i.e. contracture or surgical history.

2. Weakness and Poor Eccentric Control of the Leg Muscles:

Let's flash back to that really cool video I made… if I have weakness in my quadriceps (my front upper leg muscles), then what do I do to compensate? I turn my body and sort of go down sideways. Why?

111

Breaking Through Special Needs

Because it takes the pressure off of my quadriceps. Want to see the video? Visit https://www.breakthroughptli.com/two-main-reasons-why-your-child-might-navigate-stairs-unsafely/.

Here are some fun facts…there are THREE types of muscle contractions:

- Concentric: the one you likely think of when you think of a contraction. The muscle shortens. For example, if you lift a dumbbell up to curl, your biceps are concentrically contracting (getting shorter as it contracts).
- Isometric: the muscle length stays the same. For example, if you push against a wall. Unless you are Superwoman or Superman, you are not moving that wall. Your muscle is contracting, but not getting shorter like it did in the bicep curl.
- Eccentric: the muscle LENGTHENS while it contracts… weird, right? It is also referred to as a 'braking contraction', meaning it slows the movement down. So, let's take that bicep curl from earlier and slowly lower the weight: your bicep is eccentrically contracting as you slowly lengthen the muscle.

This one is tricky, but it is why stairs are harder to come down than they are to go up. It's also why it's a little scary watching someone go down the stairs without muscle control because it almost seems as if they may fall. When you eccentrically contract your quadriceps, they will ideally slow the movement down and prevent your knee from collapsing too fast.

I ran a marathon in upstate NY a few years ago and decided that it would be a good idea to go hiking the next day. I promise my decision-making has improved since then. During the hike, I was navigating stairs with an atypical pattern, it hurt to eccentrically contract my muscles: they were so sore. So, what did I do? I turned to the side to use different muscles, as well as both arms on the rail. This is precisely why we see some clients turn to the side, or even just rotate their legs while stepping down. Although they are likely doing this due to weakness rather than pain.

Let's imagine a hemiplegic (on their right side) client – meaning his/her left side is significantly weaker. The client will either NOT lead with their right leg – to spare the left from having to control the movement down –

Breaking Through Special Needs

OR, he/she will demonstrate a very uncontrolled and fast step down because of the weakness of the left leg. Make sense?

Now, let me be clear: there are many more reasons why stair navigation can be unsafe. Another big reason, for example, is having poor balance or coordination. Lacking eccentric muscle control during poor stair navigation relates to more movements than just stairs, and this is something we see every day here in the clinic. It is also largely why we try to focus on these types of movements during our strengthening activities, that is, so that it can promote more muscle control in the children's every day activities and promote more independence.

DOES IT MATTER IF MY CHILD CRAWLS BEFORE HE/SHE WALKS?

Developmental milestones, specifically crawling before walking, has become a topic of debate among pediatricians, occupational therapists, physical therapists, and so on. I was recently working on crawling with a client when the topic came up. Why do they need to crawl before they walk? There's evidence it may not matter, and if they skip crawling, your child can still function regularly within their environment.

Is it necessary for development, though? I'm not sure I can answer that one… however, I can mention a few things that come to mind regarding the importance of crawling and how it may make a difference if your child skips this motor milestone.

Reasons Why Crawling is Important:

1. Strength: Of course a PT would list this first. Crawling helps strengthen the hands, wrists, elbows, and shoulders, because children have to maintain activation to support the weight of their bodies. Supporting their body weight allows the ligaments in the wrist and hand to stretch and develop so that the natural arches of one's hand – which are essential for fine motor skills – can come into being. It also requires core strength to maintain balance in the "hands and knees" position, and we know how important that is! Occupational therapists may argue that non-crawlers may have more difficulty with handwriting, climbing, or pulling. Also, to keep their heads up, they must activate trunk extensors and neck extensors to lift their head against gravity, maintaining that stance while on their hands and knees. And, what does that translate into

Breaking Through Special Needs

down the line? POSTURE. If children have weak extensor muscles, or limited endurance in those muscles, they will typically present with poor posture when they are upright in sitting or standing positions.

2. Coordination: Crawling is so important for the development of coordination, and it is the very first opportunity to practice bilateral (both sides) coordination. BOTH sides of your brain must be activated to perform this task, and they must be working together to perform the reciprocal movement of crawling itself. Crawling is also a significant step for hand eye coordination. A child sees where he/she wants to go and then coordinates his/her way to the target with their hands. These types of skills, learned during crawling, can translate to reading, writing, dressing, and self-feeding.

3. Spatial/Visual Awareness: What this means is that crawling helps improve the child's awareness within their environment. Crawling can help with concepts such as depth perception, navigating obstacles, and problem solving skills.

As far as the short term is concerned, studies show that crawling is not a predictor for other early motor milestones. So, babies who do not reach the crawling phase aren't necessarily going to be "behind" in their milestones... and vice versa. Long term effects of skipping this milestone are only now being researched.

What is important to take out of this?

TUMMY TIME. There is no debate about that. Tummy time is INCREDIBLY important for strengthening those head and neck muscles, not to mention for an interaction with the environment. It's likely that your child/baby will very much dislike being put on their stomachs, though. I actually have yet to find a child who enjoys the position... BUT, it will help avoid other issues down the road, such as weakness and poor posture.

For some Tummy Time advice and routines, why not head over to www.breakthroughptli.com/resources.

I hope I've answered some of your more frequently asked questions in this section, though I realize the list is by no means exhaustive. Please feel free to reach out to me or a member of my team for more information, advice, and support.

Feel Good Stories

At our facilities, like so many across the globe, there are many children and families succeeding. I've always wondered why these successes aren't shared more frequently or in the detail that they truly should be shared. The next part of my book will focus on doing just that: sharing in depth stories of children and adults overcoming the odds. Maybe hearing these stories will give you a smile for the day or even hope that, although all of your stories are uniquely yours, there are others progressing, improving, and overcoming all odds. These stories are told from my perspective and are about the families and clients we work with; I want to tell of how they have become my family, the stories they've told me, and all of their hopes and dreams for their children. I hope that you will be able to relate to these parents and families; I want you to know that you're not alone in navigating this path and there will always be hope for more.

Gratefully, all of these families have given us permission to share their stories.

Howie

An incredibly special family entered my life a few years ago at an adaptive baseball game – I had a table set up for *Breakthrough*. I didn't know it at that point, but my life would be forever changed since meeting this family. On that day, a mom walked up to me and asked about the therapy we do at Breakthrough; she ended up telling me how she'd been looking for the type of therapy I offer for so long. She told me about her special needs son, Howie, and then called her husband Joe over with him. We talked together for a little while longer and I invited them to the office to talk in order to see if what we do would actually be a good fit for Howie. Despite that, I knew these parents were extremely motivated to help Howie live his best life.

While discussing her goals for Howie, she said the following: "Imagine if he could hold his head up while sitting… how that would change his entire view of the world!" I knew this family had hopes for a better quality of life for Howie, and I knew it was my job to help them in any and every way possible. After talking a little while longer, it was Howie's turn up at bat, and since mom and dad were the coaches, they had to go. I'll never forget that, just before Joe left the table, he put out his hand to shake mine, held my hand briefly in his, and said, "you're already like family to us, thank you. I'm looking forward to coming down to the office."

When I met with Howie's parents at the office, they allowed me to hear his story. He was born to a homeless woman, and due to her inability to care for him, he was placed in foster care. He was neuro-typical and had met all of his milestones until the first incident occurred. He was taken to the hospital because he was "sick", according to his first foster mother. He demonstrated signs of brain damage and swelling, but after further evaluation, he was sent back home. He returned to the hospital after a follow-up check-up due to suspected abuse and significant brain swelling. It was determined that he had been abused and shaken by his foster mother; he was removed from her care. After then being placed in multiple foster homes, he was later placed with a family that took care of his special needs, getting him all of the therapies and care he needed. Unfortunately, this foster family came too late, and he suffered significant brain damage from the swelling and fluid build-up from his previous abuse; he had lost his ability to do anything independently.

His mom is a speech therapist and, as if in an act of fate, Howie was placed on her caseload. They developed a special bond, and although having 4 grown children of their own, her and her husband agreed to adopt Howie into their loving family. Dad described the "home overnight visit" to me. He told me Howie was in a bassinet on his bedside, and that when he got up in the middle of the night, he looked into the bassinet to see Howie wide-eyed and looking back up at him with a smile. He told me that was the moment he knew in his heart that Howie was always meant to be theirs.

Howie has faced tremendous adversity and challenges, ones that no child should ever have to face, but thanks to the loving care of his parents, he has made so many gains since then. One of the main goals his parents have for him is for him to gain head control so that he won't need a trach to help him to breathe. When I first had the opportunity to start working with Howie, small head movements were difficult and he didn't tolerate many of the challenging positions such as sitting, kneeling, and standing for very long. He fatigued quickly, and he struggled to lift his head in these positions.

It was during one of Howie's first sessions that, when I placed him over the wedge on his belly with arm braces, he started lifting his head up to hear his favorite Barney songs. He had the biggest smile on his face and held his head up for up to twenty seconds that day.

Fast forward to now – after a massive commitment from his family and aides at home to follow through with exercises, as well as dedicated weekly visits to *Breakthrough* – he holds his head up when sitting, kneeling, and standing for nearly the whole hour session. He can now hold hands and knees without the use of the bungees – only arm bracing – for over 10 minutes long! This obviously didn't happen overnight, but it is a true representation of Howie and his family's perseverance. Despite facing so many hard challenges, and of course continuing to do so in the special needs realm, his family gave him this opportunity to do more. They held onto the hope that he will do this independently and live a better life because of it, and they will never let that go. There's a delicate balance of support and tough love when it comes to special needs children, and this family represents this in the best way possible: they will always push him for more. Why? Because they know he's capable of more. Equally, they will always be by his side to support him through everything.

I will never forget the warmth that his family brought to my table set-up on the day when I got to meet them for the very first time. I'm not even sure they realize the impact they've had on my life, but I am forever grateful to have the opportunity to be part of their family and their journey. They have taught me more about what the word "family" truly means and are – and will always be – a part of my family… forever.

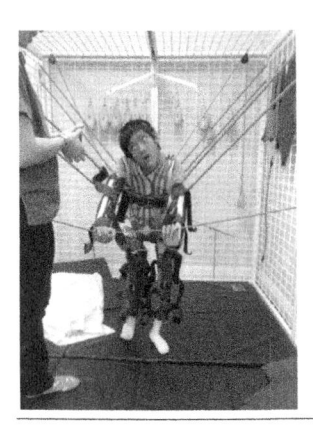

Breaking Through Special Needs

Howie, standing while lifting his head up!

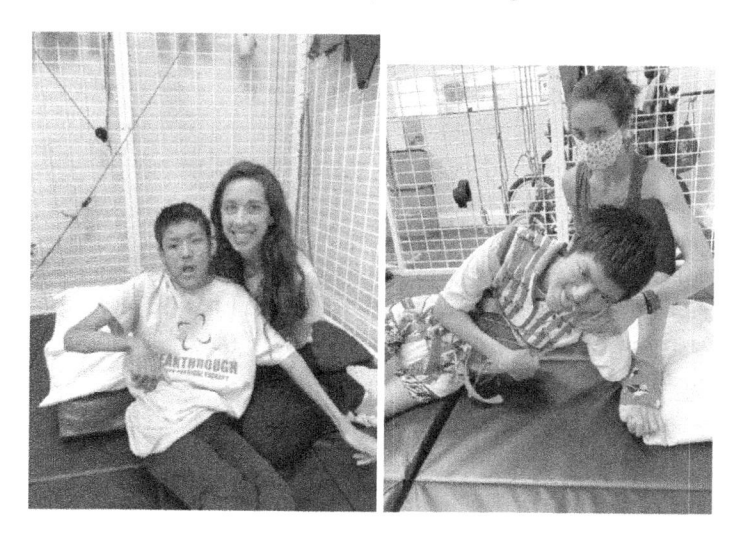

Tristan

Tristan is a 23 year old man who loves adventure and socializing. He hates staying in one place and loves getting to watch lawnmowers or landscaping, going bowling, eating out, and seeing people at his day program. I debated even writing an introduction for this guy because he is so well known by everyone – which hopefully gives you a good sense of the type of guy he is. His personality is infectious, and he's the type of guy you love to be around and hang out with. Tristan is diagnosed with Spastic Quadriplegic Cerebral Palsy and drives his power wheelchair around independently. However, he needs help with other daily activities like eating, drinking, or dressing. He and his family have been stuck with me for a while now and I wouldn't have it any other way.

Breaking Through Special Needs

I met Tristan's family over 5 years ago; I was his home therapist, as I was working for a local children's hospital that provides home services to medically fragile children and adults. I was taking over for another therapist, an occurrence which was pretty common in my time as a home therapist. I've heard horror stories of home therapists being on their phones, laptops, or showing up whenever they want, instead of actually providing care to the families they are meant to be helping.

Tristan's parents are the type of parents you love working with; they are parents that push and don't take the fact that he can't move his body the way he wants to as an excuse for poor behavior or a negative outlook. They support him in everything he needs, and they make sure that he has the best experiences and life possible, despite being wheelchair bound. They also make sure to push him outside of his comfort zone and to live with the right values.

When I was a home therapist, it was challenging only getting to see each child for a short period of time, all the while knowing that they needed so much more than what they were currently getting. Despite that, Tristan and I had the opportunity to work on sit to stand, sitting independently, keeling, maintaining stance, and so much more. It was so great to see how motivated he was to move his body, and his willingness to try new activities with me was inspiring. Tristan has an intense medical history ranging from foot surgeries, to tendon lengthening and seizures, etc., and the fact that he was still ready to give his all, each time, is incredible.

I'll never forget the day that I was working on sit to stand from the couch with Tristan in his living room. He had sand bags on his feet, my knee between his to hold stability and position, and just one little finger on his wrist for balance as he stood. His parents had just finished up work for the evening and happened to catch a glance of what we were working on. Tristan's parents were so excited to see him standing so well that mom got her camera out and took a few pictures. I absolutely loved how excited and proud they were to see Tristan working hard and standing tall. I couldn't believe how shocked they were that he could do that so well... and why he was never challenged like that before. It was a reaction I was way too familiar with, and I knew that Tristan was capable of so much more than he thought he was.

Breaking Through Special Needs

Once I opened the office, Tristan began an intensive program at *Breakthrough*. He went to day programs all day and then spent 3 hours each evening with me working really hard in his therapy. That program was absolutely one of my favorites: we rocked out on the treadmill, played "DJ" with *YouTube*, joked around, and all the while he worked on standing, walking, crawling, and all of the things doctors told his parents he'd never be capable of. The aides he had with him during his therapy sessions were also amazing and incredibly helpful in keeping Tristan motivated and the environment fun.

Tristan ended up loving the treadmill so much that he kept asking to do it. His face lit up every time he got to stand up in the bungees and take steps. So, one day, we decided to keep going and push past our normal amount of time. Tristan kept stepping and singing, we kept encouraging him, and cheering him on. That day, Tristan finished one full mile on the treadmill without a rest break. The best part about it is not only did he love every second, but he pushed and broke through so many "limits" that a man that is confined to his power chair would never be expected to do. To this day, I am so proud of him.

My most favorite day of all while working with Tristan was just a normal session, several months after he completed his program. He had worked extremely hard not to scissor his legs while trying to walk and take steps with a posterior walker and my help, but that day I challenged him more. I let go of my support and Tristan took 12 steps with the rolling walker that day… by himself. His aide *FaceTime*d his mom so she could tune in, and we all celebrated what Tristan had just achieved. You know that feeling you get when you know you just witnessed something so incredible and you want to just play it on repeat in your head? Well, I did just that, and I cried the whole way home that night. Taking steps with a walker by himself was something Tristan was told is impossible. His parents pushed him to be his best, but it was never something professionals, doctors, or therapists, ever said he'd be capable of doing. I'm not even sure Tristan was sure he would be able to do that one day, but he kept trying anyway. He worked so hard to get to that point, and he proved that literally anything is possible if you keep pushing. His perseverance and strength are the two traits I admire most about Tristan. He has been through an incredible amount of hard things, but never gave up. *His school and home therapies were never going to be enough for him to achieve*

Breaking Through Special Needs

something so great; he had to be pushed beyond what anyone ever thought he was capable of.

Tristan and his family have taught me so much over the years I've had the opportunity to work with them. Their commitment and dedication to providing the best life possible for Tristan has enabled him to push past barriers and achieve more than what anyone thought was possible. They don't see Tristan's disability as something that defines him or is an obstacle. I'm incredibly grateful to have been placed on his case many years ago in home care, as his family has become a part of my own. What I've learned from this incredible family is to never see what life throws your way as an obstacle; life is the obstacle, and you are responsible for creating your happiness within it. They don't allow anything to stand in the way of creating their life the way they want it. They've not only allowed Tristan to be the best version of himself, but their support has overflowed into my life as they encourage and support all of the growth this journey with *Breakthrough* has had over the years. They are a true representation of creating your own happiness, and that, if you push through the not-so-easy times, it can be so much more beautiful than you could ever have imagined when you get through them.

Tristan standing with our therapy dog, Chance.

Breaking Through Special Needs

When Tristan's family cheered me on at the NYC Marathon!

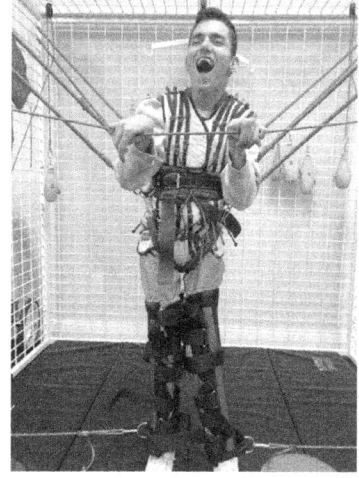

Michael

Michael is 4 year old boy who is a smiling ray of sunshine and brings warmth wherever he goes. He's the kind of kid you see and can't help but smile. A few of the first things I learned about him was that he loves to dance and earning lollipops after hard work, just like other toddlers his age. The difference for him, though, is that Michael was born with a genetic condition called Joubert Syndrome which affects the development of his brain, thereby causing hypotonia, developmental delays, visual deficits, and varying degrees of intellectual disability.

I met his family nearly two years ago when his mom reached out to us specifically looking for intensive therapy for her son. He had just

Breaking Through Special Needs

returned from an out of state trip to receive intensive therapy, during which he had improved a lot. She had learned about *Breakthrough* and wanted him to continue in intensive therapy. She had told us that her biggest goal for Michael was for him to walk, because she was told by a doctor that he won't learn to communicate and gain his speech if he wasn't walking. Mom and Dad's biggest concern was that he wouldn't be able to communicate what he needs, and they just wanted him to be as independent as possible. Michael's parents are so similar to all of our other *Breakthrough* parents in that they don't want their child to be "babied". They want him to be challenged and pushed even when it's hard. Why? Because they know he's capable of so much more.

When I first met the family, it was love at first sight. Not only was Michael the cutest little boy, but he was also surrounded by a family that so obviously wanted the best for him. As two full-time working parents, both of whom are dedicated to spending evenings taking him to therapies, they knew intensive therapy would help improve the quality of his life. Luckily, they also have the help from their extended family... who we also got to spend a lot of time with. "It takes a village", right? My first observation was that he was so close to being able to walk independently. When I held his hands to walk, he leaned backwards and relied on the support. He would also go to sit back on his bottom when he didn't feel like walking anymore. He leaned into any support he could get.

Now, yes, Michael demonstrated weaknesses and difficulty balancing, but this was not a child who didn't possess the ability and strength to walk. This was a little boy who was so held back by his fear of doing it independently that he didn't go the full nine yards. Let's think about this... he needed help and took a little longer to do many of the functional activities that just come naturally to a neuro-typical child, like rolling, sitting, and crawling. If Michael needed help to do things from when he was a baby, that was what he was used to... getting help for things.

It makes *total sense,* and we see it in the clinic all of the time. One of the best things for a kid like Michael is the bungee system. He gets to practice all of the things he's afraid to do, all without hands on him; this helps him learn the confidence that he can do it, which can carry over without bungees! It also helped that Michael has the most amazing support system at home, and I knew that anything I asked them to follow through on, would be carried over.

There was one day in particular – early on in Michael's journey at *Breakthrough* – that stands out for me. It wasn't him achieving something new or doing something great, rather, it was the day his mom received his IEP report for the year from all of his service providers. We were talking about all of his progress since he started at Breakthrough in such a short period of time – all of the small little things that make a big difference in his abilities. That was when she brought up the report. She told me about all of the reports from the different service providers, explaining that they stated all of his limitations and what he's still not able to do, but *should* be able to do. She told me that it's just so hard sometimes, because it's never the life you imagine for your child. You don't imagine your child not being able to do everything another child his age can do. She shared with me that there is just so much on her plate, and so much of her time is spent almost being Michael's personal assistant, making appointments, researching therapies, etc. rather than getting to be his mom. I know this is true for so many of you.

It can feel overwhelming, and you're left dealing with grief, stress, and worry. I was so grateful that she felt comfortable enough sharing her feelings with me that day. It allowed me another opportunity to truly see that, no matter how old the kids are, the hard parts are still hard.

Once summer time hit, Michael worked his way up to completing a full intensive program with us, completing three hours of hard work each day. He destroyed cup towers, kicked soccer balls, and even "rolled me over" with a weighted ball. By the end of it, he was crawling against resistance, kneeling with only a bungee, and transitioning from the floor with a step for his arms. He was so close to independent steps, but still nervous and leaning for support when we attempted it in the gym.

That fall, we received a phone call from mom… one that could still bring tears to my eyes. It was pretty common that whenever we got mom on the phone we talked for a while, since we are very close with all of our *Breakthrough* families. This time, mom cut right to the chase and told us that Michael got up in his classroom by himself and just walked all the way across the room without help, without prompting, **on his own terms.** My first reaction was, "What the heck!? He couldn't do that at

Breaking Through Special Needs

home, so that you guys could see it? (Kidding – sort of). We, as a team, gathered around the phone and celebrated with mom before she went on to continue the rest of her calls… and of course, I cried. They were happy tears for so many reasons: for Michael overcoming so much, and working so hard to get to that point; for being able to be part of the journey and one of the first people mom wanted to call; for the joy that you could hear in her voice as she told us. The tears, the late nights driving him to therapy, coordinating his caretakers and schedule… *it was all worth it*. It IS all worth it.

It all made sense – he wanted to achieve it on his own terms, when he was ready. And that day in class, he was ready.

What I've learned from having the opportunity to be part of this family's journey, is that, regardless of what is hard, keep pushing forward. I've learned from Michael, his parents, and his extended family, to never lose hope – continue to believe even when you can't see it happening right in front of you. *This family sees the life Michael is capable of.* They know it will be hard, but they provide him with all of the opportunities he could possibly need to achieve that. Not only are this boy and his parents a true joy to be around, but they are incredibly resilient. They choose joy and to embrace their challenges instead of fighting them. What I've learned from Michael, in particular, is that, even when you're nervous to do something, to trust yourself and to go for it. We can't wait to see what else this guy is capable of.

Breaking Through Special Needs

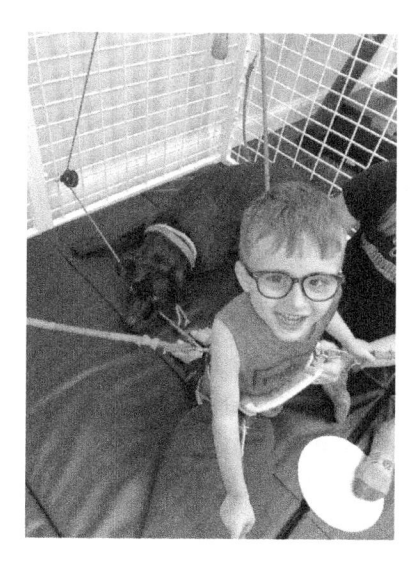

SOFIA

As I write this, Sofia is a 7 year old girl who is diagnosed with Hemiplegic Cerebral Palsy. This little fighter is the girl that I spoke about earlier in this book. Remember? She's the one I got the opportunity to watch take some of her first steps and have known since she was just two and a half years old. Sofia is the type of kid that can always make you smile. It's things like her playing music on her mom's phone so she can dance into the office and perform for us, or it's her silly faces and languages she loves to make up on the fly. Even when she was just two years old, she would sing or bring her favorite purple toys in for us to play with.

Knowing all of the smiles she brings to the people around her, you would never guess her medical history is as scary as it is. Sofia suffered a hemorrhage in her brain in utero and had to undergo several brain surgeries for Hydrocephalus and shunt revisions. All of this caused Sofia to present with left sided weakness and neglect. Mom was on the hunt for ways to help her daughter be as independent as possible. At the time when I first saw her, Sofia hated to be put onto hands and knees or onto her belly. She had difficulty with a lot of everyday activities and movements, and mom wanted her to be the two year old she thought she would be: running around, exploring her environment, and being independent.

Breaking Through Special Needs

Mom was told by multiple doctors and therapists that "she has CP, that's just the way it is" when referring to her level of abilities and what limitations she currently faced; mom wasn't happy with that answer. She was determined to help Sofia get stronger and improve all of the activities she had to do on a day-to-day basis, including walking, stair navigation, and getting up and down from the floor. She just wanted her to experience life the way she should, and not to be held back by her physical limitations. So, Sofia was scheduled to undergo SPML surgery, that is, Selective Percutaneous Myofascial Lengthening. At the time, her left leg had rotated completely in and it limited her ability to walk safely, so mom sought help and advice on how to help correct what was going on. She was seen at our office after clearance from the doctor for intensive therapy: all of the positions that were difficult for Sofia to perform, all of the gait abnormalities she presented with, we could help correct with the use of our knowledge and ability to help children into positions they normally wouldn't be able to attain.

When she showed up at our office post-surgery, Sofia had difficulty, again, with getting up from the floor, bending to pick things up from the floor, and navigating steps and stair cases. She also presented with a walking pattern that made it easy for her to trip and fall. Even positions that you and I can attain – and likely take for granted each day – such as half kneeling, which is kneeling with one leg forward, Sofia struggled with. Luckily, because of the amazing use of our pulley system with weights and spider suspension, we were able to put her into half kneel to practice lunges; we could also have her stand on uneven surfaces that she typically wouldn't be able to stand on, all while being in a safe environment and WITHOUT having hands on her.

I often find that so many of the kids, because of their weaknesses and constant need of help to do things in their everyday lives, lack a lot of confidence in themselves to be able to perform independent activities. They'll reach out for your hand, or will wait for you to assist them getting up from the floor. Why? Because it's what they are used to. Sofia would display these tendencies when getting up from the floor, stepping onto a small step, or even walking up an inclined surface. With the use of weight assisted treadmill training (up an incline, of course), and a variety of strengthening exercises, floor to stand transitions in the bungees, and step practice, Sofia gained the ability to step up and down onto a step without any assistance... all by herself. Eventually, we were able to

Breaking Through Special Needs

challenge her with weights at her feet, as well as in other ways. She even gained the ability to get up from the floor without the use of her hands... independently!

Now, all of that sounds great, right? Ultimately, what that has led to is what so many parents tell us they want for their child: **Sofia being as independent as possible and giving her the best shot at doing all of the things the doctors told her family she wouldn't be able to do.** Thanks to her parents' commitment and whole hearted dedication to providing the best opportunities for Sofia, combined with Sofia's determination and perseverance, it has led her to being able to do so much that, for a long time, they weren't sure she would ever be able to do. She even knows how to make it incredibly fun, whether she challenges her therapists to do cartwheels if she does something right (for her own entertainment, obviously), or she dances her way into the office while playing fun music.

Although she doesn't request her purple lollipops anymore, Sofia has defied so many odds, and every day is an example of perseverance and resilience. She teaches us more than we could ever teach her, and we have been so grateful to be part of her journey as she continues to achieve new benchmarks!

Breaking Through Special Needs

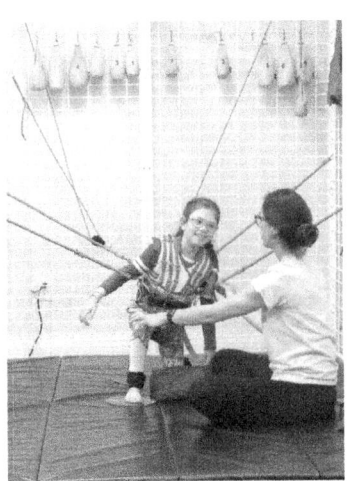

Me and Sofia when she was just 3 years old!

HENRY

Where do I start with this guy? I guess I will start with the fact that I have never met a kinder, sweeter, more genuine soul than his. He's the type of person you love to tease and joke around with (or maybe that's just me), but that you look forward to seeing no matter how frequently it is. He's the person who burns you a CD filled with music that he thinks you'll like, or types up a letter just to say thank you and how much you mean to him. He's the guy that, whatever I tell him is happening in the office, always wants to help in any way he can.

Henry is a 52 year old man diagnosed with Spastic Quadriplegic Cerebral Palsy. His journey at *Breakthrough* began over 2 years ago when he wrote me an email asking if we are able to help adults and not just younger children. He had heard about one of his friends attending our facility for physical therapy, and being the type of person he is – always wanting to push himself and move his body – he reached out to us.

You may think Henry's story would be different because he's older, but just like so many of the other families we work with, Henry and his family just wanted to provide him an opportunity to move his body freely and independently. When it comes to our older clients, I so often hear the following: "Do you think this would still help him/her?", "Will this still benefit them?", "Is it too late?" There may be some things about an older client's condition that we might not be able to change, whether that is a contracture or positioning, but here's the thing:

Anyone can make progress no matter what their age is.

I have worked with countless adults who have made tremendous progress despite their age. It is the consistent effort to move, perform therapies, and practice their skills that make the difference. I compare it to any typically developing human from childhood to adulthood. As a child, you are involved in so many different activities, you are more active and 'on the move'. As you grow into adulthood, though, many adults go to work, take care of their families, and have lost much of the "active" movement they used to have. Many stop exercising, stop being involved in group activities, etc. I see many of the same things with a special needs adult. Often, when their special needs child is younger, parents will involve them in so many different therapies and activities. However, as they get older, those things get less and less. Movement isn't as encouraged when they get older. Additionally, parents and caregivers age too, therefore making it a challenge to keep up; it's especially challenging when it comes to lifting or transfers.

Breaking Through Special Needs

And yet, despite Henry's age, he has remained motivated, and his loving family has encouraged him to participate and continue being the best version of himself. He is involved in horseback riding at a local ranch, too, where he attends his work program.

I remember his first visit to *Breakthrough*. His mom and sister watched as we did many different activities and positions. I put Henry into a hands and knees position with braces to help his arms. At this point, he was breathing heavier because it is a very hard position to hold, and we attempted reaching with each arm. He did a few reaches and I told him I'd give him a rest break. I remember him telling me "no"... immediately. I did a double take and asked "what did you just say?" He repeated, "no", and that he wanted to keep going, moving, and reaching. I knew from that moment that we had a really special guy working with us. He didn't want to give up just because he was tired. Instead, he wanted to push a few more repetitions and give it just a little bit more. Why? Because he was so happy to simply move.

It was months into working with Henry that we got to learn about him even more, come up with challenges, and find a way to use his mental toughness to get the most out of him. He started to tolerate so much more, hold positions for longer times, and even did dynamic exercises that challenged him. He came in one day for his normal session and told us they were even starting to notice changes at his program for horseback riding: that he's sitting taller, his balance is better on the horse, and even that his legs are looser getting onto it. How incredible is it that these improvements have made something he absolutely loves to do – horseback riding – a better experience for him? Those are the stories I love most, because it means we've made an impact in another area that he loves; we've been able to assist him to improve the quality of his experiences. In fact, his family has never seen him as excited to do something before every PT session; they have seen his sessions help him with so many things. Henry explains that "whenever my hour of PT is over, I always wish I could stay and do more because I enjoy it so much." My heart is so glad that he is so comfortable and happy here with us.

Henry continues to make progress, and every small feat is a large gain for him. He has a toughness and positivity that inspires everyone around him. Oh, and he also has a competitiveness that is unmatched... he is always up for a challenge. He especially loves to challenge everyone in

Breaking Through Special Needs

arm wrestling competitions, though that's mostly because he always wins! What I love most about Henry's story is that he never gives up and he always maintains an attitude that *failure comes from not ever trying*. He is always up for every challenge we throw his way and he continues to persevere through what so many see as his limitations. He's an inspiration to everyone he meets and fills our hearts with his positivity and genuineness. Henry is proof that the only limitations you have are those you place on yourself. We are forever grateful for having the opportunity to work with Henry and his incredible, loving family, and are thrilled to see what barriers he breaks through next.

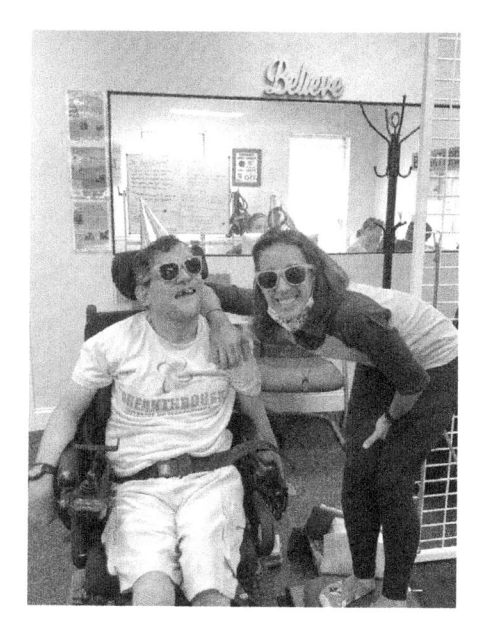

Breaking Through Special Needs

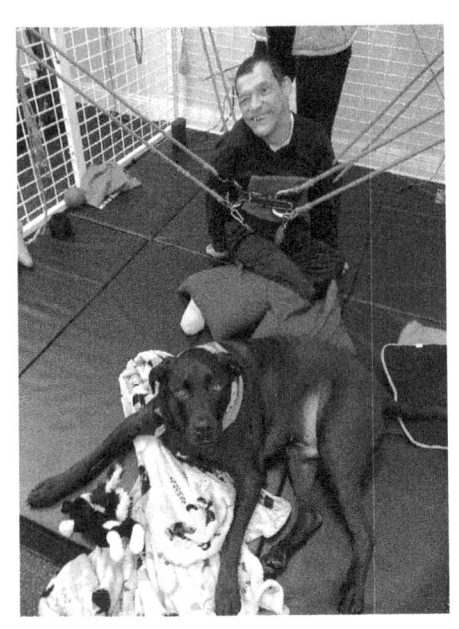

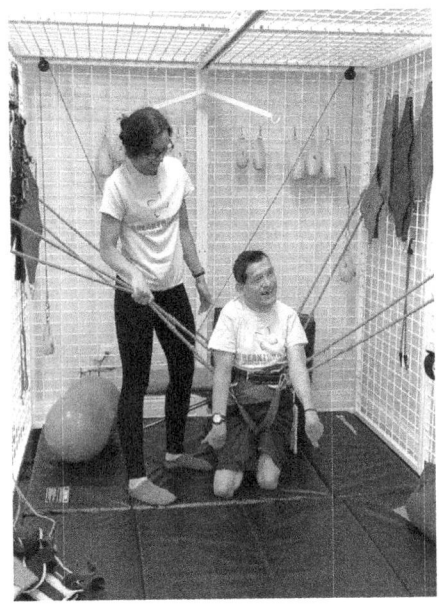

Savvy

Savvy is a happy 5 year old girl – wait, correction… the happiest little girl who is diagnosed with Spastic Quadriplegic Cerebral Palsy. She is a ball of smiles and laughs, and she has the special ability to brighten anyone and everyone's day. A few of the first things I learned about Savvy were that she absolutely loves Elmo and that she has a very special bond with her mom. I met Savvy and her mom over two years ago, when she reached out seeking alternative therapy for her daughter.

I remember one of my first conversations with her mom; she told me all of the therapies, treatments, and outlets she's tried with Savvy in order to try and give her the best life possible. She said, "you never know, so I'd rather try it because who knows where she would be without it?" When I first met them in person, I knew we would be able to help them. From prior experience working with kids just like Savvy, and speaking with her mom, I knew she would be capable of so much if she was just given the opportunity.

It was at Savvy's evaluation that we hit our first bump in the road, though. You see, Savvy has a hard time adjusting to new places and new people, so when we started, all of the games and silliness in the world couldn't calm her down. During a few of the first sessions we tried, we only got to 20-30 minutes in, because Savvy was still having a hard time adjusting. Soon, however, she started tolerating the full hour, and session after session she grew more accustomed to coming in and playing. She started enjoying her time in therapy, and now it's hard to get her to stop laughing and smiling. One of the most incredible parts of all of that, though, is that, as hard as it was for mom to continue bringing her daughter in and seeing her scared and trying something new, she continued to try anyway. Why? She knew that, if this has the ability to help her, it is worth it. I'm not a parent myself, but I've worked closely with so many of them that I have seen just how incredibly challenging taking this leap of faith really is.

During one of the first times I was worked with Savvy, her mom opened up to me about her full story. She explained what happened when Savvy was born. Unfortunately, it is not the first time I've heard a story like hers, that is, one where multiple doctors and specialists have failed a family in need of answers. Here is her story:

It started at her 32 week gynecologist visit when she worriedly told them that she could not feel the baby. The doctor told her it was because she was small, or maybe that the placenta was in front, but that she'd do a sonogram during the next visit at 34 weeks. That visit never came, because Savvy was born prematurely. She did not have enough platelets: mom's were attacking hers, and she had the umbilical cord wrapped around her neck. Savvy suffered a brain hemorrhage requiring transfusions and immediate care, so her parents weren't even able to meet her until the next day. She was at the hospital for about 25 days.

After she was sent home, the pediatric neurologist sent Savvy for MRIs and EEGs, with a referral to a developmental pediatrician. They never gave her any diagnosis, but stated "we won't know what she cannot do until she doesn't do it." Early Intervention started right away, and yet another developmental pediatrician never gave the family a diagnosis. It wasn't until the second physical therapist from Early Intervention suggested a developmental orthopedic, that answers were forthcoming. The developmental orthopedic finally gave Savvy the diagnosis of Spastic Quadriplegic Cerebral Palsy at 18 months old. Only then did a doctor finally give them answers and take the time to explain what it meant and where to go from there.

Failed by multiple doctors, they never gave up. Her parents were committed to finding answers and finding help. The part that is

Breaking Through Special Needs

unacceptable is the lack of answers and empathy. Worried, frightened, anxious parents arrived at these specialist offices after a traumatic experience from birth, and yet nobody sat down with them to point them to resources, what to look for, or what the future might look like for their beautiful little girl. Instead, they denied this family answers and came up with poor excuses for an inability to tell the family a hard answer. Savvy's diagnosis does not change her condition, but what it does change is her parents' understanding of what's going on and what they can do to help her.

After they finally received the support they deserved, Savvy's parents got her involved in whatever they could find, including help from a special education teacher, taking her to speech therapy, hippotherapy, and aqua therapy. Eventually, they found *Breakthrough*. Savvy even received stem cell treatment in June of 2019 prior to her first intensive program with us. Not only did Savvy participate in a full intensive program with us at *Breakthrough*, but she *loved* it. She laughed, smiled, said new words, and made tremendous progress. She went from only being able to sit by herself for about one minute, to sitting independently for seventeen minutes. She was able to hold hands and knees by herself, start pulling herself in crawling, and stand for long periods of time without getting tired. When I first met them, Savvy was only able to say a few words; she learned the number "eight", so we only counted to eight repeatedly. We always took eight steps, counted eight repetitions, and stacked eight blocks. Now, though, she says so many words and phrases that have allowed her to express her needs; she can even request a different *Dora the Explorer* song to play during therapy time.

Savvy's progress does not surprise me one bit. And that's not because of the amount of therapies her parents have gotten her involved with, but because of the resilience and perseverance her parents have demonstrated during really tough times. No matter what, her mom searches for therapies, trials, and professionals who will help her daughter live her absolute best life. Of course, Savvy will have the same outlook on her life that they do, too: to keep pushing.

What I've learned from working with this family is to never give up; have an attitude towards life that means you go find the answer you need, even if people tell you no; not to simply accept what you're given, but to find what you deserve. So many families have been failed by doctors,

Breaking Through Special Needs

healthcare professionals, other family members, friends, or teachers, etc., but the important thing to remember is that you never have to accept what you've been given. There are always more people out there who will be able to help. It doesn't seem fair that it always has to be a fight for you – you have to advocate and find the best doctors for your child – but, the alternative isn't necessarily something you want either. I truly admire Savvy's mom's view on her challenges. She's not afraid to fight. She's not afraid to speak up for what she wants for her daughter, and she never, ever gives up.

When we asked her about her experience at *Breakthrough* a while back, she said: *"If we had given up, we wouldn't be where we are today. We really had to stick it through; quite a few weeks I doubted coming as well, but now looking back I'm so glad that we did, because she's made so many gains in her abilities. To sit, to crawl, to take steps with a walker... she wouldn't have been able to do that if I gave up."*

To witness this family's resilience and commitment is inspiring. I'm not certain they are aware of the impact they've had on my life, but I am forever grateful to have connected with them and to be able to watch Savvy's progress as she pushes through more barriers.

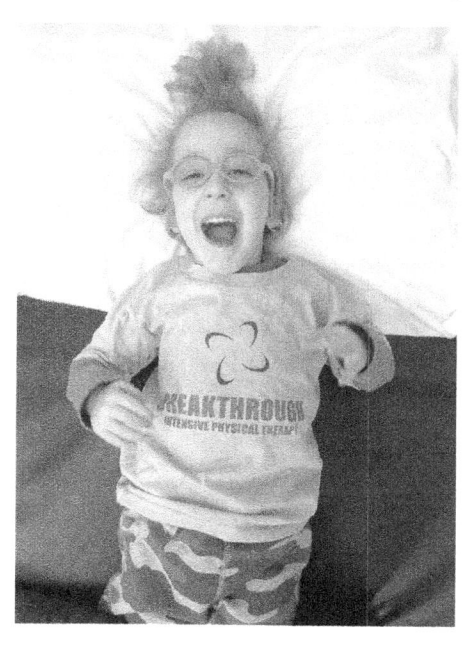

Breaking Through Special Needs

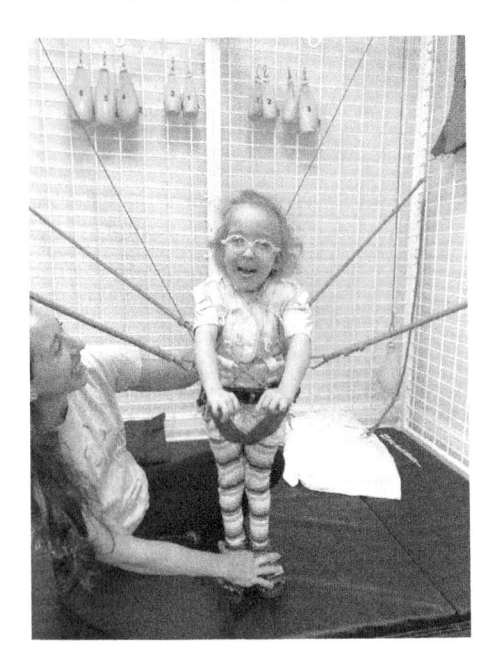

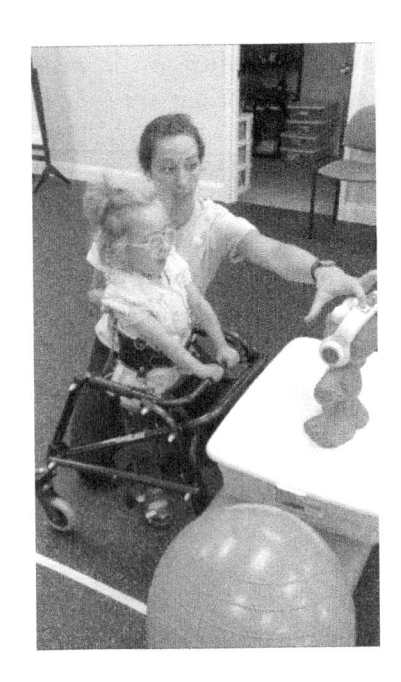

Maddie

Maddie is an incredibly motivated 6 year old girl who loves waving and saying hi to everyone she meets.

Due to complications during labor and delivery, she was diagnosed with Dyskinetic Cerebral Palsy and hypotonia, which means her body has a lot of involuntary movements and she has difficulty attaining and maintaining functional positions by herself. Maddie knows exactly what you're saying to her, but has to overcome her own body to do what she really wants to do. Aside from loving to help mom out around the house with baking, cleaning, or watching some of her favorite shows, Maddie loves to practice her exercises… by herself… with no help from anyone. She's the kind of kid that us PT's love helping. Why? Because you never have to tell her to practice… she just does it! She may be little, but I've never met a little girl more determined than she is, and I'll tell you why.

When I first met with Maddie's parents, they were concerned that her school therapies just weren't enough. They told me they weren't sure what she's capable of, or if it was even possible, but their number one goal for her was to eventually sit by herself. I remember them asking me during her evaluation if I thought it was possible; if I thought that she would eventually be able to sit all by herself one day. We get this question so often from all of the parents we get to speak with… "Do you think for someone like her/him, that it's possible for them to do (insert goal) one day?" I often find that, because these children are not always challenged enough in their school or home environments, or progress can be more like a roller coaster than a straight line, that parents aren't sure what to expect from their child They've gotten so used to doctors and professionals telling them all of their children's limitations, so how would parents know what's possible? Doctors are constantly telling them their child will never speak, or walk, or be able to hold their head up by themselves… so, the line gets blurred between "this doctor doesn't get it", and "they're the professional, what else am I supposed to believe?"

I'll never forget the day mom and Maddie came into the office for their regular session, and after catching up on how their week was, I had asked mom how a neurology appointment went. Maddie was seeing a new neurologist, and after spending barely any time with them in the office, she told Maddie's parents three words: "she's not cognitive". How that doctor came to that conclusion, I will never understand. Horror stories like this, doctors and professionals like that, who continue to make sure the special needs children are not heard or seen, make my blood boil. She obviously lost them as clients immediately, but how many other families and parents did she tell that to? How many other children did she say things like that in front of? How many parents went home after visiting with a doctor like her and felt hopeless, because if professionals and doctors don't believe in their child, who will? I know that not only Maddie's parents have experienced this: so many of you reading this have had similar heartbreaking stories.

Despite Maddie's parents denying the doctor's outrageous claim, it still hurt them, for obvious reasons. To hear that from a doctor about your own child, one who has gone through so much more than any child should, is hurtful. It's hurtful when people see the world in a negative light. If that doctor spent one minute speaking with Maddie herself… if she just asked how she was that day, or said hi and saw her wave back with that beautiful smile she greets everyone with, then she wouldn't have even been able to say that.

From the first day I got to challenge Maddie, I knew she was a tough, determined little girl who was not going to let anything stop her from doing what she wanted. Not only was she ready for every challenge I put her up to, but she even tried helping me with all of the equipment. She even pulled the TheraSuit over her shoulders to help me put it on her.

However, when she first got to sit up in the bungees of the Universal Exercise Unit, she needed arm bracing to help her keep her arms straight; she also needed help at her body so that she could focus on lifting her head. No matter how many times her head would collapse forward, though, she always lifted it back up… even if she couldn't hold it there for very long. We used to count how many seconds she was able to hold her head up for in each position. I always reminisce with mom about those first sessions because of how far she's come since then.

Maddie now can sit by herself, with the bungees, while playing games and completing puzzles. She pushes herself up from the floor to sit up against the couch to watch TV with mom and dad for entire lengths of episodes. She even hands mom toys while she's sitting up and mom is folding laundry on the couch. This girl literally never stops practicing her new abilities and skills. Even through the night mom catches her practicing pushing up to sit, time after time… after time. No matter what, this girl is incredibly motivated to move her body the way she wants to, with purpose – independently. She now even commando crawls around her house all by herself and has an independent means of mobility! I've worked with so many children over the years, and they all possess a desire to move and push past their own bodies' restrictions.

The most rewarding part of Maddie's journey so far has been to witness her tenacity and perseverance. No matter what situation you put this girl in, she tries anyway. Maddie just needed to be given the opportunity to learn and push past her current level. She needed the encouragement and the belief in her from those around her in order to realize that she is capable of so much more. What I've learned from watching and growing close with her parents matches Maddie's outlook. No matter who tells you "no" or "can't", always find people who say "yes" and "can". It takes so much strength and perseverance to overcome all that they have been through; they remain hopeful that the best is yet to come for their little girl. Their sacrifice, and the love that they pour into Maddie's life, has allowed her to blossom and be who she was always meant to be… a fierce, independent little girl with limitless potential.

Breaking Through Special Needs

Dino

Dino is a 5 year old stud who loves music, silly noises, and being around the people he loves. He has a smile that melts your heart, and has the type of personality that makes you want to just snuggle him. He is diagnosed with Cerebral Palsy, Microcephaly, and Epilepsy. He has overcome multiple seizures, requiring long periods of time in the hospital, and has faced regression. Despite the most challenging times, Dino has made incredible progress and his family has taught me so much: I had to include his story here.

I first spoke with Dino's mom during the first winter that *Breakthrough* was open, and I still remember that entire conversation. When I first spoke with her, she told me all about Dino and what he was able to do. When I asked her what her goals were for him, she replied with something that I hear so frequently from parents: she doesn't know what he's capable of, but she just wants to give him the opportunity to do more and be his best. She expressed that his home and school therapies were good, but she wasn't sure if they were enough for him. So often, there exists a fear in parents that they are not doing enough for their child, or that they are missing out on progress and gains. However, it wasn't like that for Dino's parents: they were motivated to challenge him and give him opportunities to move his body and learn.

I remember sitting down with Dino and his parents for the first time in *Breakthrough*'s gym – back then, the walls were barely decorated and it was just me, myself, and I; not even Chance was an employee yet (our therapy dog). We had the opportunity to connect, discuss Dino, and I could show them what our therapy at *Breakthrough* really looks like, as well as what to expect. Just after that appointment, Dino endured another intractable seizure and was hospitalized throughout the winter and into the spring. After he recovered, I finally got the opportunity to start working with him early in the summer.

When I first got Dino in the equipment, we started working on sitting, holding hands and knees, and even weight bearing during standing. I would have to use my entire body over his to prevent him from thrusting backwards; I also had to hold his arms down. He had a lot of difficulty putting weight through his arms and keeping his head upright in any position. Soon, we started celebrating him holding his head up for longer

Breaking Through Special Needs

periods of time, and he started to hold his hands down and pushing weight through them to hold himself... without the use of arm bracing or me as the PT. He started holding his back up, and he even held his knees straight. And, as long as we were making music or singing the itsy bitsy spider, he had a smile on his face. Flash forward to now and he is sitting by himself up to a minute with his head up; he's pulling his body forward when crawling, and he's even taking some steps with weight assist!

Watching him grow and progress through everything he has faced has taught me so much. Realizing how hard it was for him to just push through his arms, or to lift his head up, and having to go through such challenging sessions, to seeing what he is capable of now, is nothing short of incredible. What is also incredible is his family's commitment and dedication to helping Dino be his best. While watching Dino work hard every single week has taught me so much, it has been him and his family that has *changed me* and why I wanted to include his story for others to read. Not only have his parents dedicated every week to his time at *Breakthrough*, but I've been able to meet grandparents, aunts, and uncles, too – all with the same attitude towards Dino: unwavering support, love, and pride.

I didn't realize it at any particular moment, but this family became part of my own.

They define what family truly means, that is, a combination of love, support, encouragement, and helping one another be their best selves, despite challenges. They don't second guess decisions on family – they're automatic for them. It is no surprise that Dino is overcoming so much in the environment they've created for him. It's an added bonus that being part of the family also means they take Chance for walks during therapy sessions, or Dino's little sister, Ella, cuddles and plays with Chance the entire time.

What I've learned from having the opportunity to work with this family is to maintain a positive perspective on every situation, no matter what; to have a positive outlook on life no matter what you may be facing. I admire them because they just keep going and don't take the little things so seriously. They are un-phased by setbacks, and have created joy in every hard situation. Dino is bound for so much more because of their perspectives and commitment. There is enough challenge to help Dino

Breaking Through Special Needs

be his best, but there is also a tremendous amount of love. How lucky am I to have a family like this grow with *Breakthrough*?

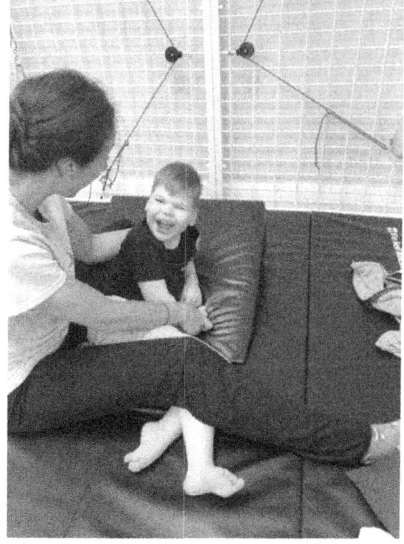

Charlotte

Charlotte is 13 year old girl filled with tons of sass and so much love. She is diagnosed with Tuberous Sclerosis Complex, of which you may never have heard, but is a condition where benign tumors grow in the body.

Breaking Through Special Needs

Charlotte happens to have them in her brain. She is also diagnosed with Epilepsy, facing numerous seizures per day despite medications. She has overcome multiple brain surgeries to remove these tumors, and is now is a fun loving teenager who enjoys swimming, dancing, and being around her friends and family. She lights up at the simple things, and has an incredible sense of humor that makes being around her continuously fun – even with her sass!

I met Charlotte and her mom about a year into *Breakthrough* opening. I still remember the first conversation I had with her mom over the phone; we spoke about why she was seeking more therapy for Charlotte. You see, Charlotte absolutely loves being around her cousins, friends, and family, and as she grew, it became more difficult for her to move her body the way she wanted to. I remember mom telling me that, instead of playing with cousins, she would sit in a chair on the side; that navigating the stairs in their home was challenging for her, and that she needed help to get up and move around the house.

Her mom explained that they just want to give her every opportunity possible to be the best version of herself; they want her to have the quality of life she deserves. Her parents are determined to give her the best outcomes and to help her do the things she loves to do, all without feeling held back by her own body. It was at Charlotte's Discovery session that we met for the first time, and mom and I talked at length about these things, that is, what she really saw for Charlotte. When I say at length, I mean it. She was my last appointment of the day, and we sat there for two hours not even realizing how late it was until Charlotte's dad called to ask where they were. It was the first time her mom and I both cried while talking together, but it was most definitely not the last.

Charlotte receives related services in school, including PT, OT, and speech therapy, but her mom felt like it wasn't enough for her – she felt Charlotte needed to be challenged to do more. We hear this every single day at *Breakthrough*: the 30 minute school services are just not enough to make meaningful gains. We also hear about the frustrations that come with setting "school related goals", and the lack of communication between therapists and parents. One day, Charlotte's mom came into the office after Charlotte's IEP meeting; she was exhausted. I wish I could say that wasn't the norm, but so many parents are emotionally drained when it comes to being a constant advocate for their children. We talked about how it went, and how she had to fight for Charlotte's services because her OT was trying to decrease them. Now, I'm in no way saying this therapist was doing something wrong by trying to decrease her services based on clinical judgment in the school setting. *What I am saying is that the system has failed these families.* Charlotte presents with weakness all along her left side and has very limited use of her left arm.

How on earth do we have a system where we can make a clinical judgement that a child does not need therapies when she does not have any functional use of her left arm? Why did Charlotte's mom have to fight to not have Charlotte's services decreased?

Unfortunately, the system says that, if the children can meet their "school related goals", then they don't need services anymore. Part of me understands that Charlotte's school therapist is just "following the rules", but the other part of me so strongly believes that irrational rules shouldn't be followed, and that it's up to us as service providers to break the system which undermines these families. The unfortunate part is that it's not the only time Charlotte's mom has had to advocate so strongly for her daughter. This is one reason why Charlotte's parents sought more therapy: the current system doesn't push their daughter to be her best and most independent self.

Once we started working together, you could see how much Charlotte loved movement. A few of her favorite activities are jumping in the bungees and walking on the treadmill. One day, I tried to challenge her by having her walk backwards on the treadmill with the bungee assist. Regardless of how I tried to help her, she wasn't able to stay up and step fast enough, or far enough, so that she could keep going. About 9 months later, we tried it together again and she was able to do it with a little bit of assistance… for up to 30 seconds. Flash forward to now and she continues to make progress; she can now go over 3 minutes long without stopping. This example of Charlotte's improvement defines the type of person she is: a fighter who is determined to keep pushing. I will always remember the smile on her face when she was able to walk backwards for the first time, and how proud of herself she was that day as we cheered and clapped for her. It's wasn't only backwards walking that she improved, but also her stair navigation, her endurance, her floor to stand transitions, and so much more.

Breaking Through Special Needs

Back in 2018, I fundraised for a foundation called Share the Voice while training for the NYC marathon. Share the Voice gives away adaptive trikes to children and adults with special needs in order to provide recreational opportunities that every child should have. I fundraised enough for two trikes, and Charlotte was the recipient of one of them. The organization always surprises the recipient with the prize, and this makes it so special! In this case, we got the bikes delivered to our office and I built them with my sister, Michelle. At Charlotte's next appointment, we hid one of the bikes in the equipment closet and later rolled it out and surprised her and her family... just in time for Christmas! Of course, we cried a little bit, but my favorite part of this wasn't the excitement Charlotte had, or even the smiles it brought that day: it was the pictures Mom sent me of their family cycling together... the first time her sister Aubrey got to ride her bike with her big sister. And, it will bring so many more smiles for their family than just that day, and that makes me so incredibly happy and proud.

The most rewarding part of Charlotte's journey is how her family says it's impacted their lives. Her mom told us a story that one day her, Charlotte's dad, and Charlotte's little sister, Aubrey, were sitting on the couch in one room in the house while Charlotte was in another. Charlotte got up from her seat – herself – and walked over to sit with her family... something she wouldn't have been able to do prior to all her hard work and progress.

What I've learned from working with Charlotte and her family is that support doesn't mean there aren't challenges. Charlotte's parents support, encourage, and are her biggest cheerleaders, but they still want to provide her the opportunity to be as independent as possible and enjoy her life. And that doesn't come without challenging her to push further, longer, and to try things she's never tried. This family defines "tough love", because her parents realize that sometimes you need to push through the hard stuff to get to where you really want to be. I've also learned that you do whatever it takes for your family, even if that means having to fight for them and do things you're not always comfortable doing. I'm forever grateful for being able to witness their resilience and demonstration of love, support, and encouragement in every aspect of their lives. I'm especially grateful to have them as part of our family, and to watch Charlotte's progress as she overcomes more barriers, thereby proving that she is capable of so much more.

Breaking Through Special Needs

Charlotte, Mom, Aubrey, and I when we surprised her with her trike!

Breaking Through Special Needs

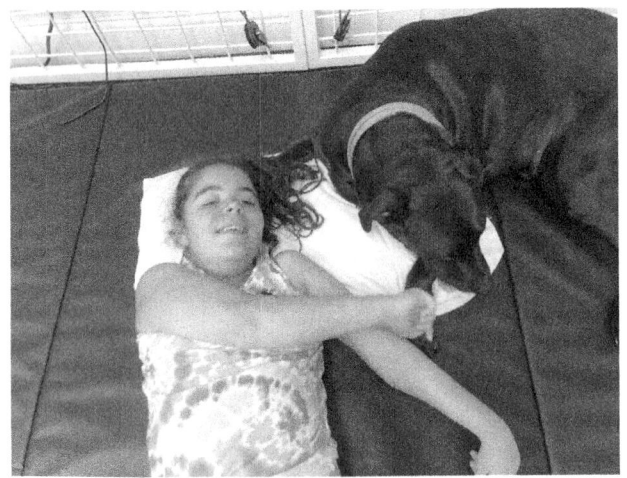

SEAN

Sean is a fun-loving 12 year old who has a smile that fills your heart. Sean is diagnosed with Autism and ADHD and became part of our *Breakthrough* family a year ago when his parents looked at alternative ways to help him get healthy. Like so many kids with Autism, Sean has sensory issues; this makes it extremely challenging to eat healthily, and so he had a lot of difficulty managing his weight. He also has weakness and muscle tightness that makes physical activities harder for him. His parents were understandably concerned, knowing that his lab results were completely out of range for a child his age. I speak with so many parents with similar concerns. Parents have difficulty finding programs for their child in

148

which he/she will *want* to participate, ones that give the children enough time and attention to actually help them through so that they can improve.

To keep doing something, or participating in something, you have to find success in it, right? Think about yourself, for example. All of the things you weren't really good at, you've likely quit or they're not part of your life anymore. All of the things you've found success in were more enjoyable, and you've likely participated in them for longer periods. I know that's true for me, and it's true for these kids as well. They need to find success and joy in the difficult things so that they will continue to try and make an effort to participate and improve. So, it's no surprise when these children don't want to participate in sports or physical exercise: it's hard for them, or they feel unsuccessful. It's easier to want to play video games or sit and watch television on the couch. Physical exercise is especially challenging for them, and it has proven to be extremely difficult finding programs that incorporate physical exercise that the children actually enjoy. So many of these children and adults are less motivated. Why? Because it's so hard for them, and they'd rather stay in their comfort zones. Even participating in sports is daunting to these children and adults.

I have never quite seen two parents encourage their child like Sean's parents do. When he first started coming, they would participate and help guide him during the class, all the while encouraging him *and* the other kids. When he wanted to give up or said he was tired, even though they knew he was struggling and they knew it was hard for him, they pushed him to finish anyway. Not only did Sean get pushed to reach new levels, but he was also able to make friends in class.

I'll never forget when his mom called the office to tell us about Sean's most recent doctor's visit. It was three months into him participating in our group fitness program, and his parents took him for updated blood work and labs. The results were astounding: his numbers had come down significantly, both regarding his liver and his blood sugar levels.

Not only were his labs improving, but his strength, flexibility, and even coordination were gradually getting better as he accomplished new exercises successfully, even as they became more challenging. What I believe to be one of the most important shifts in Sean concerned his

Breaking Through Special Needs

confidence. He often gets down on himself, and he gets frustrated as he tries new exercises or activities that are challenging. He used to become fussy and demonstrate his clear frustration with himself as he attempted new activities. Now, when we throw new things Sean's way, he tries no matter what. He's gained the confidence in himself to always give his best effort... even if it's hard.

Then quarantine hit.

It was the most stressful, challenging, and overwhelming time for all parents, but especially for parents with a special needs child. You all **immediately** turned into teacher, mom/dad, employee, and therapist, and you still had to manage day-to-day activities. Routine was flipped upside down, stomped on, squished, ripped up, and every other type of demolition adjective there is. But, what happens when these children (and us, essentially) thrive off of routine? What happens when they don't understand that things have to be different right now?

Well, let me tell you something, all of our *Breakthrough* parents thrived. Not only that, but they managed – no matter how challenging it became. Especially Sean's parents. Sean struggled with the switch to virtual school and programs that involved a lack of routine and socialization. That didn't stop his parents from pushing to get the most out of him, though. When things were stressful, they pushed harder. They did not for a single second stop; they didn't allow fear or anxiety to creep in and inhibit all of the progress Sean has made thus far. And you know what? His parents continue to show up two times a week to participate in our Bootcamp classes, and Sean has continued to thrive and make progress. I'm so proud of this family.

Sean's mom confided in me and explained that watching the classes is sometimes quite hard. She told us that she cried watching Sean struggle, because it was so hard for him. And, knowing that he was doing his best, but seeing his frustration, was heartbreaking for them as parents. That is exactly what is so special about them, though. As heartbreaking as it can be to watch your child be challenged, you still know what's best for them, and you encourage them to push through the hard stuff. I'm not even sure they realize the incredible example they have set for him with their perseverance throughout such a challenging time. They have been such an inspiration to myself and our team at *Breakthrough*.

Breaking Through Special Needs

There have been so many new perspectives that I have learned from working with families. The biggest one I've learned from Sean and his parents is about love: there doesn't have to be "a balance" between *tough love* and *support* when you love someone. Those two concepts can be intertwined with one another, and you can refrain from giving the one you love what they want in the moment, knowing that, if they push through the hard stuff, they'll gain so much more. Sean's parents have pushed him to do so much outside of his comfort zone, and this has ultimately allowed him to flourish and succeed. I have learned incredible lessons watching them work with Sean, both in-person and virtually. They've made the best of a heartbreaking situation, and despite hard times, for them, family is family: if you keep pouring love into something, you receive it back. We are so incredibly blessed to have a family like Sean's as part of our *Breakthrough* family, and I know that with their continued love, support, and encouragement, there are no limits to what Sean will be able to accomplish.

Sean and mom, Victoria, at our annual holiday party.

Breaking Through Special Needs

CADENCE

Cadence is yet another story of resilience and perseverance. She is a 14 year old girl diagnosed with a rare genetic condition called Fox G1. This condition causes her to have constant movements and hypertonicity, along with other challenges including seizures. Cadence is another one of our very special clients that can light up the whole room with her smile. She loves everything girly: including getting dressed up, shopping, and of course girl time with mom. She especially loves the beach, music concerts, and watching her daddy surf the waves. During her time at *Breakthrough*, she has formed an incredibly special bond with our therapy pup, Chance, who always motivates her while she reaches to pet him.

I'll never forget when I first met her parents and they described their current lifestyle with Cadence. Two incredible parents sat across from me and told me of the challenges they faced throughout Cadence's lifetime, from battling insurance companies, difficulties getting equipment, doctors who just want to jump to surgery without listening to them, all the way through to having to jump through hoops for certain services and nursing care. The list could continue to go on, but I'm certain that, as you read this, you've been there, too. Unfortunately, they still face these kinds of challenges, as you all do, but with the system the way it is, and the neglect exercised by our healthcare system, to get what your child not only needs, but deserves, is always a fight.

I sat there and listened as they told me about the times Cadence would have a seizure and turn blue and they were desperate to get their baby girl help. They told me about the times Cadence faced anxiety, and because she's non-verbal, they weren't able to gather what was wrong. They told me about the times the doctors told them that there's nothing they can do, that Cadence won't be able to do anything by herself. Despite this, and although those incidents have made a significant impact on their lives, they also told me about the most important stories: how, despite a scary circumstance, Cadence always has a smile on her face. They told me about the times when they didn't let difficulties with traveling get in the way of their family vacations, or when they got to go backstage at concerts to meet some of her favorite bands. This family allowed me to see into their lives... the good and the not so good times. They allowed me to see that it's not so hard for you, as parents, to balance negative experiences with positives. Why? Because even if you can't always can see the positives right away, you *look* for them… even in the really scary times.

We talked for a really long time, as this family allowed me to know their past, present, and what they see for Cadence's future. Over time, Cadence's movements have caused a severe scoliosis, and they had been told by multiple surgeons that she may need hip and back surgeries due to her movement disorder. So, when I asked what their ultimate goals were for her, they wanted to avoid surgery if at all possible. Major hip and back surgery is scary in general, but add in complications from her diagnosis, as well as her movements, and then it's understandable to see why they were terrified. Although they are happy with her new school and therapies, they knew she needed more.

I always say evaluations with our families are my favorite part. Not only do you get to see the look on the children's faces as they stand by themselves for the first time (even if assisted by bungees), but you also get to see the look on the parents' faces too. If only I could freeze frame every reaction to include them here, but at least they're engrained in my memories.

During Cadence's evaluation, we worked our way up from the floor, testing every single position and movement until we got to standing. I strapped some bracing on her legs, raised the bungees higher to help bear her weight, and voila, Cadence was standing by herself. I was behind her to make sure she maintained her foot positioning, and I had the best view in the house. I watched as her parents videoed, took pictures, and shed some tears. They said they couldn't believe how tall she was, and boy, did she stand tall that day! I turned to look at Cadence's face only to find the biggest, most beautiful smile as she stood so proudly. There was no anxiety that day, no fighting with doctors, nobody talking about the limitations she will face… just hope and happiness: hope that she will avoid surgeries, hope that she will one day stand on her own, and endless hope for a better quality of life because of it.

We were working with Cadence for a few months and she was putting in such hard work each week. Her school therapists transitioned her to a gait trainer to work with her, and then it happened… Cadence took steps in her gait training for the very first time… all by herself. I remember when her mom first told me and showed me the video, and if you know

Breaking Through Special Needs

absolutely anything about me at this point in the book, you know I cried. You see, it took Cadence so much hard work to take a step. If, for one moment, you sit back and realize that accomplishment – which I know you can – you'll know why I cried. It's incredible.

Months after that, Cadence and her parents went to the hip surgeon again for their next check in. They were scared that she may have to now face surgery, but guess what… the doctor told them she doesn't need it! After seeing multiple back surgeons, the ultimate decision was that she doesn't yet need a spinal rod either. This isn't to say she may never need it, but the efforts her parents have made, the work her school and home therapists put in, all in combination with her involvement with more weight bearing through her therapy with us at *Breakthrough*, is working to help Cadence have the best quality of life possible: a life where she shouldn't need to face surgery and one in which she can be herself, a teenage girl who loves all of the things girls do at that age.

Getting the opportunity to be part of this family's journey has truly enriched all of us at *Breakthrough*. It's humbling to know this family trusts us with their daughter's care, but it's also been a journey of togetherness. It's so much more than just the physical therapy Cadence receives. It's the check-in phone calls, hearing about their fun trips, and all of the other avenues of support with which we have grown so close to this incredible family. With Cadence's parents' perseverance and tenacity to give her every opportunity they can, this girl is off to living the life she deserves, and we love getting the opportunity to be part of it.

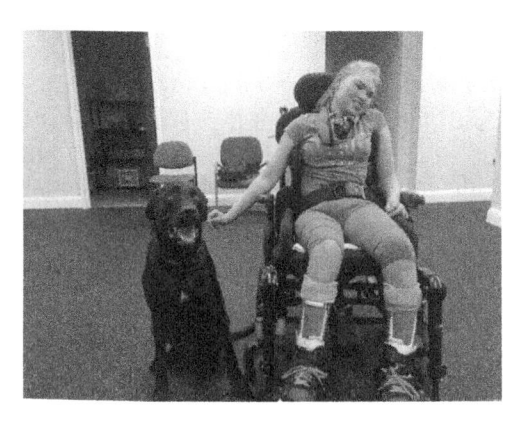

Breaking Through Special Needs

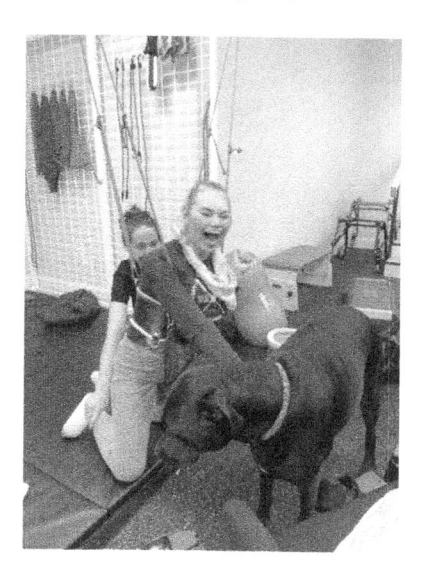

Cadence working hard to pet Chance!

Dad (Jason) and Mom (Gina), with Cadence at our annual holiday party.

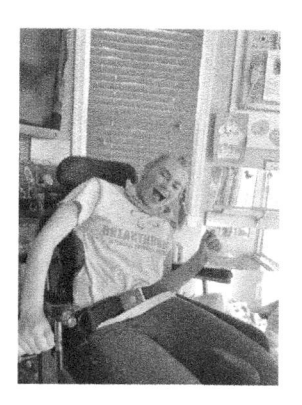

Final Thoughts

Over the twelve months that it took me to write this book, there was one iconic speech that kept lingering in my thoughts: Martin Luther King Jnr's, "I have a Dream". I thought about how brave his words were, how he spoke of his vision so resolutely – a world without segregation, without racism, togetherness despite religion or the color of your skin. And then I thought about his words in relation to our community. What if there was inclusion for all, that is, inclusion for the special needs community, both physically and mentally disabled children and adults.

What would a world like that look like?

It would be nice to think that we are there right now, but we are far from it. Not only does our environment pose challenges in the form of inaccessible areas or lack of accommodation for wheelchairs and walking aids, but I think the biggest challenge to overcome is society's view of the special needs population itself. The term "special needs" already suggests that these families, children, and adults, are defined against a preconceived "normal". So many of the challenges I hear parents and siblings speak of are all related to a lack of acceptance, a lack of funding, and a lack of attention to truly help this community succeed. Services, programs, and funding are always slim for this community, and what happens when funding is cut higher up? The programs for the children and families who need it the most are affected. The first programs cut when a budget gets tightened are the ones related to special needs.

Recently – here in New York – funding was cut from a program that provides care at home for families. Agencies that help provide care for medically fragile children had funding cut, therefore negatively affecting many, many families. While I do realize anyone who feels strongly about a program or particular population of people will feel a decision for a budget cut is unjust, but what about when it cuts into how families are able to care for their medically fragile children? What happens when families no longer receive help within the home and are unable to keep up with demands of providing for their family and maintaining safe spaces and services for their children? What happens then?

Breaking Through Special Needs

What would the world look like if families – just like yours – were able to go out without having to check websites or call ahead to make sure the area is accessible? What if it just was? What would it look like if everyone treated your children like the humans they are instead of staring, making rude comments, or being bothered by your family's needs? What would the world look like if you didn't have to fight for services, equipment, or your child's basic rights?
It seems like a far-away land people only dream about, or write about in books, but I do believe a world like this is possible.

I have a dream that one day people will treat others with pure kindness; that the differences within this community are embraced and not seen as a challenge to overcome.

I have a dream that one day society will not label the disabled community as "special", but essential. They will be noticed, they will be acknowledged, they will be given resources, and treated with true empathy.

I have a dream that one day people will see there is no one life that is less valuable than another's, regardless of physical or cognitive capabilities; that each individual will get an opportunity to succeed, despite having more – or fewer – support services than another.

Our society was created for the "typical" child to succeed. Our schooling system, healthcare system, and social system all accept the current idea that "special needs", or different needs, is less than the norm. Our schooling system is designed for children who all learn the same, and advance their knowledge at the same rate and speed. Our healthcare system is designed to fail individuals in our community – "ongoing care" is maintenance. Our social system and environment is designed to keep those with alternative needs out, that is, to lack space and accommodation for accessibility. People stare at those who seem different to themselves; they are agitated by someone with Autism paying for their own grocery bill and taking longer than usual, or they stare at a family when they have their child in a wheelchair at the aquarium. Our society was not created for those with different needs, and now comes the long process of weaving our community into "the socially accepted" community and belief systems.

Breaking Through Special Needs

But, it is possible. One day, together – as a community – we will get there, and the world will finally see the light, joy, and love that this community can bring. The world will see the strength, tenacity, and resourcefulness this community possesses. One day, they will realize that the special needs community makes us whole and complete, and without them, life would not offer all of the beauty it does.

I hope this book gave you answers, support, and peace. Your child, and you, are immensely special. I wish the very best for you all and I hope – in the very near future – that we may meet in person.

With love,
Christine

Breaking Through Special Needs

Practicing Gratitude

To my Breakthrough families. You have inspired me and touched my life more than you know. You are my family and the reason I wake up each morning excited to pursue my mission. I am forever grateful to be part of your journey. Thank you will never be enough for what you have given me.

To Kevin. Thank you for believing in me even when I doubted myself. Your support, encouragement, and gentle push to be outside of my comfort zone, is the reason that Breakthrough is even here. No matter what I dream up, you always believe it's possible for me, and you continue to help me reach those goals. Thank you for making me a better version of myself. I love you.

To my family. Mom and Dad, you have given me more opportunities than many get in life, and you are the reason I am here, right now, able to follow my dreams and serve this community. Michelle, not many people would tolerate their sister as their boss. Thank you for your constant belief in me, your passion to go above and beyond, and for being my best friend. Joe, Brenda, Jav, and Mike: thank you for your endless support and encouragement.

To my team at Breakthrough. Thank you for believing in me as your leader, and thank you for your consistent effort and passion to pursue our mission and vision. No matter what crazy ideas I bring to the table, you're always on board and trust my intentions to roll with it. I am incredibly grateful to each of you for your commitment, compassion, and all you've done to go above and beyond for our community.

Lastly, to everyone else who has played a significant role in my journey; my coach, Paul Gough, for your guidance and challenge to see the world differently and help me get out of my own way to create this community; my friends – Crystal and Jackie– for your constant support and belief that I can do whatever I set out to do; Nancy – for not only being my accountability partner, but a friend to celebrate the ups and push through the downs; and Brooke, Annie, Payal, and Cody – for challenging me, balanced with support to help me get to where I want to go.

There are so many people who have played an important role in my journey. I would not be who I am today without these very special people in my life. We are just getting started, people!

Made in the USA
Coppell, TX
29 January 2021